Rubber Stamping

BEYOND

the

BASICS

By Michele Abel

Author of **The Art of Rubber Stamping Easy as 1-2-3!**

ISBN 0-9630756-1-6
Library of Congress Catalog Card Number: 94-74042

Cover and text design by Pam Sussman/Genesis Communications

Text illustrations by Michele Abel, Howard Friedman

Art direction by Nancy Jordan

Product photography by Paul Reiling Photography

Printing by Palmer Printing, St. Cloud, Minnesota

Inquiries and orders should be addressed to:
Publishers Distribution Service
121 East Front Street, Suite 203
Traverse City, MI 49684
1-800-345-0096

OR

Creative Press
3000 St. Albans Mill Road
Minnetonka, Minnesota 55343
1-612-483-0329

5   4   3   2
97   96   95

Acknowledgements

I want to thank all those who've given their time, support, and advice, including Carla Barrett, Vicky Betthauser, Pat Niemuth, Suze Weinberg, Dee Gruenig, Charles Bandes. A special thanks to my friend and art director, Nancy Jordan, who went above and beyond for me; to my husband, Michael, and to Hilary Jordan, who both gave up the use of their homes for book production!; to my son, Howard Friedman, who took care of the technical and production problems; and my daughter, Stefanie Friedman, for all her advice and support.

The following manufacturers were kind enough to donate products and advice that allowed me to experiment, and develop the many stamp ideas found within: EK Success, Carlstadt, NJ; Enchanted Creations, Hawley, PA; Fiskars Corporation; Craft-T Products, Fairmont, MN; Hero Arts Rubber Stamps; Rubber Baby Buggy Bumpers, Fort Collins, CO; A Stamp in the Hand, Carson, CA; Judi-Kins, Gardena, CA; Hot Potatoes, Nashville, TN; A La Art, Cleveland, OH.

The illustrations used to add a touch of whimsy are from Art Parts, Orange, CA, electronic clip art available for Macintosh and PC. Most of the images can also be found in rubber through Rolling Bay Rubber Stamps. Rolling Bay, WA.

For information on how to get a listing of all companies offering rubber stamps and related products, please see the coupon at the back of the book.

Table of Contents

Preface

This book will take us beyond the ordinary. As promised in my first book, rubber stamping is truly as "easy as 1,2,3" once you know the basics. I have found rubber stamping to be an ever-increasing source of creativity because of all the ways to enhance "artwork." This book will take us beyond the basics to new artistic techniques that add beauty and style to our stamping.

▲ ▲ ▲

The art of stamping continues to flourish. Although some people used to consider stamping a fad, or child's play, it seems to have survived the test of time. Why? Because, I believe, it is an art form, or an art tool. It's a creative outlet for "artists," and "non-artists" as well.

Why Stamp?

And, the ever popular debate: Is stamping Art? There are styles and techniques in this art form, just as in other art forms. It is possible to blend the art stamp designs in order to make a visual statement, or just for pure artistic creativeness.

A rubber stamp is not art, just as a pencil, paint brush or a bag of clay is not art. Stamps are the tools to making art, just as surely as any other art tool. Look upon stamps as tools. Don't worry about keeping them looking like new, if that's not your thing, just stampable.

Stamps allow us to express our thoughts, feelings, and emotions. Stamping is only limited by our imagination and talent to express this with stamps. Don't worry about "mistakes"

while stamping. Often the best creations are "interesting errors." Some of the best ideas start out as "mistakes."

▲ ▲ ▲

Inspiration

As you put stamp to paper, it often has a mind of its own. You don't always create what you set out to do. One idea or inspiration will give birth to so many others. Sometimes the original idea gets totally discarded in favor of some tangent that's discovered in pursuing the original. We put something of ourselves in our work. The stamps we choose, the colors we work with, the subjects we pick. Our work will change over time, as we change. Because we become better at stamping, but also as we change as individuals.

▲ ▲ ▲

Thank You

I would like to thank all the wonderful people I have met, the unforgettable stampers at rubber stamp conventions, all the fun, creative people in classes I have taught, the store owners I have met and talked with, and the great rubber stamp company owners. The creativity that flows whenever stampers get together is something non-stampers cannot imagine. I truly think that rubber stampers are some of the nicest people I know.

I said in the first book, that rubber stamping is a healthful addiction. From a talented rubber stamper, and fabulous calligrapher, a great poem that I think says it all:

Ode to Rubber

I think that I shall never see
My life return to normalcy.
A life where rubber had no part
But now whose mention thrills my heart,
And keeps me thinking all the day
Of how I can find time to play.

A life where I am free to think
Of other things than stamps and ink.
And life was calm, and life was quiet,
But I saw a stamp, and I HAD to buy it.
And the rest, as they say, is history —
I don't have stamps...my stamps have me!

Peggy Crowe
aka Calli Grapher
January, 1992

Okay, time to dig in and play with some new and fun ideas that will take you beyond the basics...

These books have a special binding that allows the book to open and lay flat. This will keep the book open to the page you need as you're working.

Easy as 1,2,3

My first book, *The Art of Rubber Stamping, Easy as 1, 2, 3* divided the basic elements of stamping into 3 distinct and easy steps: stamping, coloring, and decorative add-ons. These steps are the basis for virtually all stamping we do. We may only use one or two of these steps, or our finished work may be very complex. But the basics of stamping remain the same.

Stampers have insatiable appetites for more skills to add to their stamping. Let's go back to the basics, and take a look at the options and techniques used to vary our stamping.

Step 1: Stamping

There are two elements in this step: the inks we use and the paper we stamp on. First, let's look at the various paper choices we have, as the paper will dictate some of our ink choices.

▲ ▲ ▲

Papers

PAPERS. Whether you truly appreciate fine paper as some people do, myself included, or whether you just use paper as a medium to stamp on, there are some basics you should know. The feel, the texture, the look, and the color of various papers will all affect the final stamped design. There are certain papers that give stamped images a crisper look, others will create a softer look. The inks you stamp with are affected by paper. The markers, pencils, watercolors all change their look with the papers we choose. Not all papers can handle all mediums of stamping. The texture of the paper may determine what you do with your design.

Most stampers tend to use plain, white cardstock. As I became more creative with my own stamping, I began to look at papers in a different way. I could see wrapping papers, tissues, decorative paper bags, maps, newspapers, cardboard, as another medium to expand my stamped designs. Keep in mind when choosing papers that even thin papers can be used to stamp on, although you may have to mount it onto card stock.

Use the paper you begin to collect. Experiment. Don't let your paper just collect dust. How else do we know which papers will work for us? Buy handmade papers, papers with fibers, papers with patterns, origami papers, rice papers. Buy papers, and play with them. Stamp on them. Tear them and use them in collages. Layer with them. Try different coloring techniques and mediums. Discover what you like working with.

HOT TIP

Save your scraps! Small, odd shaped scraps will come in handy someday. Have a box or drawer to store all your paper scraps.

▲ ▲ ▲

All paper has a *grain*. Grain direction refers to the direction in which individual fibers run in the formed sheet of paper.

The grain may not be that important when stamping on paper you don't intend to fold. However, if you need to fold paper, it should be folded with the grain to give your projects a neat appearance. Not knowing which way the grain goes can result in uneven edges and/or cracks along the fold line. The importance of this step depends on the paper. Heavier papers, and papers with definite grains will be affected more.

HOT TIP

When gluing two or more sheets of paper together, the grains must all go in the same direction whether or not the paper is folded. If they don't, pages will buckle.

To determine the grain, do one of the following:
▲ Bend a large sheet of coverstock edge to edge, then open and bend the opposite edges together. The paper will bend most easily with the grain.
▲ Take a small section of your paper and rip in each direction. A sheet will tear more cleanly with the grain than against it.
▲ *The Wet Test*. An easy way to find the grain, especially with linen papers and those where the grain is not readily

Going With the Grain

PAPER BENDS EASIER WHEN FOLDED WITH THE GRAIN

PAPER WILL NOT BEND EASILY WHEN FOLDED AGAINST THE GRAIN

CURL

apparent:
- Cut a small square of paper, about 1" square, from your paper.
- Be sure to make a mark on this piece as to its orientation to the larger sheet.
- Wet one surface of the piece.
- Set it down. It will curl in the direction of the grain.

Once the grain is determined, plan your project so that most of the folds are with the grain.

▲ ▲ ▲

Scoring Paper

Scoring Paper. You can crease most of your lightweight and medium-weight papers by hand. However, heavy-weight papers and cardstock need to be scored. To crease, test to be sure the paper will bend easily without cracking at the folded edge.

To hand fold:
- ▲ Place the paper on a hard, flat surface.
- ▲ The line of the crease should run horizontally in front of you from left to right across your body.
- ▲ Take the edge of the paper and roll up to whatever position necessary to form the crease.
- ▲ To get the straightest fold, the crease should always be at the bottom of the paper, not at the side or top.

Tools needed to score:
A straight-edge (ruler), and one of the following scoring tools, such as:
- ▲ **Bone folder.** A flat piece of bone or plastic with one curved and one pointed (but not sharp) end. This is invaluable for creasing, folding and smoothing paper.
- ▲ **Burnishing tool.** One end is a metal ball for scoring, the other end is the flat edge folder.
- ▲ **Embossing tool.** Used for dry paper embossing, it has a

wooden or plastic handle with a small metal ball on either end.

▲ **X-Acto ®blade**. Lightly score on coated papers to make a clean fold. Be careful not to cut all the way through.

▲ **Mechanical lead pencil, or ballpoint pen,** WITHOUT the lead or ink down, can be used.

▲ **Regular kitchen knife.** Use the backside of the blade.

To score:

▲ Place your straight-edge where you intend your crease to be. You will be scoring along the inside of the fold.

▲ Make indentations along the score line with your scoring tool.

▲ Make as many passes as you need to get a definite, crisp line.

▲ Turn the paper over and fold. Use the long edge of the bone folder to make a nice, sharp crease.

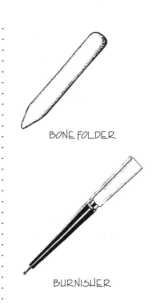

BONE FOLDER

BURNISHER

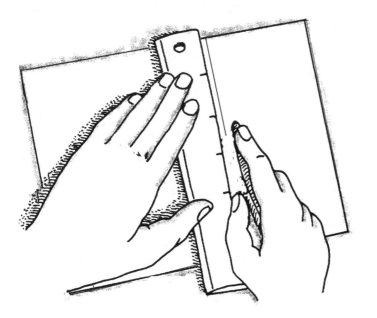

Paper
Paper
Paper

Manufactured papers and cards give you a flexible and color-ful base for your stamped creations.

▲ ▲ ▲

COATED PAPERS

GLOSSY. Glossy papers can be clay-based, such as Champion Kromecoat® and King James Cast Coat. Dye-ink, markers, and pigment ink can all be used on these papers (though pigment inks must be embossed. More on this later.). Glossy papers can be found where stamps are sold.

There are also oil-based glossy papers, such as Astrolux and Plastisheen. These papers come in a rich, wonderful array of colors. However, you *must* stamp and emboss on these papers as they will not accept inks without embossing.

MATTE. These are coated papers that do not appear glossy. They are known by such names as Mattecoat™ and Kashmir® and have the same properties of the glossy clay-based papers. For example, Mattecoat paper, from Judi-Kins, is made from 50% recycled paper. It has a smooth, matte finish, is acid-free, and produces a crisp, clear image everytime you stamp. Unlike Kromecoat, the ink does not pool on your stamped designs. To prevent smudging when coloring in your image, give the ink a minute or two to dry.

▲ ▲ ▲

UNCOATED PAPERS

Uncoated, matte-finish papers have a greater absorbency than the coated papers. Most inks, markers, and colored pencils can be used with these papers, as well as watercolors.

Texture also plays an important part with uncoated papers. The smoother the texture, the crisper the stamped image will be. Each paper has its own personality, so experiment with all different textures so you will find ones that you like to work with.

HOT TIP

Make friends with your local printer. They generally have boxes full of scrap papers they throw away every day.

WATERCOLOR PAPER. There are different grades and textures of watercolor papers. These papers work well with watercolors, watercolor pencils, and Marvys.

Rubber stamps work the best on the smoother watercolor papers. The more texture to the paper, the less surface to work with. Therefore, you will get better results using small stamps. A little grass stamp will stamp beautifully, whereas a large butterfly stamp with much detail will not completely stamp on the more textured papers.

BRISTOL PAPER. An economical paper designed for a broad range of drawing and painting media. Bristol is available in a wide range of cardstock weights. It stamps well, and takes to watercolors.

RAG PAPERS. These papers contain a high percentage of fiber from cotton or linen fabrics, including recycled clothing. The percentage of rag indicates the amount of cotton used in making the paper. The more rag, the higher the quality and the price of the paper. Rag papers are commonly used by artists for watercolors and etchings.

ACID-FREE PAPERS. This refers to the acidity or alkalinity quality of a paper. Acid-free papers are those from which all acids have been removed during manufacturing to improve strength and color. These papers, with a PH count of 7.07 and higher, are not as likely to disintegrate with handling and storage. They should not yellow or become brittle. Manufacturers are going more to acid-free papers now because they share our concern with the environment. There is less pollution created in producing these papers. Also the mills are also able to produce a "whiter white" with the acid-free paper.

ARCHIVAL-QUALITY PAPERS. When doing a project that you will want to last, such as a photo album, look for achival-quality. These papers will not disintegrate, become yellow, or brittle with age as quickly as other papers. Rag papers with a high percentage of cotton, and high quality acid-free papers, are just such papers to use.

▲ ▲ ▲

PHOTO ALBUMS

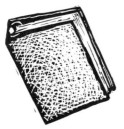

PHOTO ALBUMS. Stamping in photo albums gives a personal-ized touch to the albums and adds interest.

Use stamps to add borders to the page. Or border individual pictures. Theme stamps, such as birthday, Christmas, travel, etc. will tie together the pictures on a page or pages. For an interesting touch, use old-fashioned photo corners to attach photos to the page, or make your own album and use very heavy paper, or lightweight mat board. Cut diagonal slits on the page, then slip the corners of the photos into the slits.

The best paper to use for albums is acid-free archival paper. You can also use binders that are acid-free, acid-free storage boxes, and even ballpoint pens specially made for use with the acid-free papers.. These and many other products are available by catalog from Lasting Impressions, Rochester, New York.

▲ ▲ ▲

HANDMADE AND SPECIALTY PAPERS

MULBERRY PAPER. Comes in a wide variety of textures and colors, containing long fibers that create a delicate, feathered edge when torn. Thickness varies from lacy, tissue weight, to sturdy, heavy-weight. The texture may be smooth, rough, or crinkled and may contain embedded bark, leaves or contrast-ing color accents.

Mulberry paper will tear better if you first run a line of water along the tear line and soak.

You can stamp directly onto the smooth mulberry papers or use them to layer with other stamped or decorated papers. The feathered torn edge of these papers shows up beautifully against a contrasting background. Gold and silver embossing powders are especially dramatic on the darker colors.

Bends and wrinkles may be removed from these papers with a warm steam iron. Some colors, especially reds and purples, may change color when heated, but will return to their original color when cool. Note: Do not iron the lacy, white paper with gold and silver specks. This paper is not made from mulberry fibers and will melt.

ORIENTAL SPECIALTY PAPERS. These papers have a smooth surface and clean cut edges which makes them excellent for stamping. Most of these papers also work well for stencil or heat embossing, brayers, or laser printing. Lace papers are white with lacy patterns formed by jets of water sprayed onto the newly formed sheets. When a brayer is used on this paper, the lace paper is dyed, and the underlying paper is left with a beautiful lace pattern imprint.

FLOWER PETAL PAPERS. Hand-made in India, they contain real flower petals and grasses. These papers work well with all types of stamping, heat embossing or stencil embossing. The natural look of these papers makes them an excellent complement to the mulberry papers.

MOMI. Heavy papers with a hand crinkled surface are too textured for stamping. These look beautiful in a collage with stamped pieces.

TAKE NOTE

Handmade and specialty papers sometimes react differently to inks, paints, and adhesives. Be sure to test techniques on a small practice piece.

▲ ▲ ▲

OTHER PAPERS

GLITTER AND HOLOGRAPHIC PAPERS. Adhesive-backed, self-stick glitter and holographic paper comes in many different colors and patterns. They are oil-based, or plastic, and can only be used with pigment inks and embossed. The surface is too slick, and will not take a dye-based stamp pad.

These papers add fun touches to a stamped card, and work well with layering and borders. Glitter and holographic papers can be found in stores that sell stamps and accessories.

HOT TIP

When embossing, use the heat gun very carefully. It's very easy to melt or burst the paper, so stop heating AS SOON AS it is embossed. Let it cool down before touching it.
Caution: when cutting out the embossed image, do not cut through the embossing. The embossed design will flake off.

ACETATES AND TRANSPARENCIES. Wonderful see-through papers for special effects.

▲ **Wet Media Acetate** by Imagemaker Films comes 12 sheets to a pad. The acetate is coated on both sides, accepts wet art media including inks, watercolors and markers. You may also write directly on the film. To stamp on acetate, this is the one to use. You can stamp on other acetates as well, however, wet media acetate works the best. Use a permanent ink to stamp the image on any of the acetates.

▲ **Transparency paper**, available in office supply stores, is also good for stamping. There are transparency papers made for *copiers* and others made for *laser printers*. They are treated with a heat stabilizing process and made to withstand heat.

TAKE NOTE

Transparencies for laser printers are made to withstand the heat of laser printers, which can get as hot as 350°. This makes them ideal for stamping with pigment ink and embossing, as they will take the heat of the heat tool. Regular acetate, on the other hand, will warp when embossed.

HOT TIP

If you have trouble with embossing powders clinging to the transparency paper, wipe with a fabric softener sheet first.

To color stamped images on acetate, I prefer to use Zig Projection Twin pens. These pens are meant to be used on transparencies and the colors are bright and clear. Clean Color II Pens, by Zig, and fabric pens, will color on the acetates as well; however, the colors may not appear as vibrant. The pens are permanent and will not smear. For writing directly on film, you can use transparency pens, Sharpie® markers, or a dip pen with Higgins Black Magic ink.

▲ **DRAFTING APPLIQUE FILM.** Another type of transparency paper is an adhesive-backed, pressure-sensitive paper called *Drafting Applique Film*, available in both matte and glossy. Use the matte finish for stamping, copying and coloring. (See more in *High Tech Stamping* chapter.)

Corrugated Creations

A fabulous technique, shared by Louise Muensterman and Jeanne Haley of southern California, uses corrugated paper for putting stamped designs directly on the paper. The design goes in and out with the corrugated ribs:

1. Use large paper scraps. The paper can have a stamped design, be patterned paper, postoids, postal stamps, tissue paper, etc.

2. Use a glue stick (not a wet glue).

3. Set the design on the corrugated paper, and use the round stylus of an embossing tool to get the paper to stick in the corrugated ridges. A bone folder works well along with the stylus.

4. Allow space visually for the shrinkage of the paper scraps, as the ridges reduce the size of the paper.

Big, Bold and Beautiful

Use designs stamped on sticker paper for very bold, vivid images in your projects. Stamp, or stamp and emboss, with bright, vivid colors. Cut out all the designs and layer them on your project. You can layer on layer, overlap and make your design as lush as you like. There is no need to worry about masking when you use sticker paper!

The bigger and bolder your images, the bigger and bolder the impact. I look for the solid rubber stamps that can be stamped in solid, bright colors. This technique adds color, interest and texture to your work.

MASKING PAPER. There is a sticky-back product made especially for masking, called Mask-It by Pressing Matters. It is removable and re-usable. It stays where you put it and can be re-used over and over. After using, stick the mask on a glossy-coated card stock to save for future use.

VELLUM PAPER. A sheer, see-through paper that can be used for stamping. Since vellum smears easily when first stamped, give it time to dry before coloring in. Once dry, the ink is permanent. You can emboss, cut out and overlay on a stamped design. Great for the wings of a butterfly, etc. Use vellum paper with stained glass images, too. (See more under *The Stained Glass Look.*)

LAMINATING SHEETS. You can buy clear plastic self-adhesive sheets of paper made expressly to laminate paper. This is considered "cold laminating," as it needs no heat for the sheets to adhere to the paper you are laminating. There are also laminating machines that will do laminating with heat, and some that will do both hot and cold laminating.

If you have stamped art work that you want to save, and do not want to fade with time, use the laminating sheets for this. It will also give your paper more weight, if you need it. The advantage to cold lamination is you can laminate images that have been embossed, and photos, which you can not do with heat.

STICKER PAPER. Sticker paper can be found in both a matte and glossy finish. It comes in various brand names, such as "Crack and Peel." Sticker paper has a back that peels off, and can be adhered to any surface, I will refer to it often throughout the book, as it is a paper that can be used for many things.

ODDS AND ENDS. Check out wallpaper and wrapping paper. Depending on the coating, some can be stamped on directly.

Stamp on sticker paper and adhere the designs to papers that are coated.

Combine stamped images with color photographs, illustrations, comics, etc. You can come up with some wonderful surrealistic backgrounds this way.

Cardboard, corrugated boxes cut up, and corrugated papers all can be used. If you can't stamp on these surfaces, use them as wonderful backgrounds for your stamped cards.

Tissue paper works well in collages. It comes in a myriad of colors, as well as patterns, florals and lace.

▲ ▲ ▲

The Stained Glass Look. Stamps with large interior spaces work well for a stained glass look. In fact, some companies carry stamps specifically designed to create this look.

There are different techniques to get this truly unique look.
▲ The simplest way to get a stained glass image is to stamp a design on a colorful *magazine page*.
  • Stamp in black, and emboss in clear.
  • The color from the magazine gives the look of the stained glass.
  • Cut the image out, and mount on cardstock.

▲ Use *vellum paper*.
  • Stamp the design in black ink on the vellum.
  • Turn the paper over and color on the back, to keep ink from smearing.

▲ Use *stained glass paints*. (available at craft and art stores):
  • Stamp your image in black pigment ink on *transparency paper made for laser printers* .

THE STAINED GLASS LOOK

- Emboss with clear embossing powder. (Preheat your heat tool before using to help prevent warping.)
- Let cool.
- The embossing will keep the glass paint inside the lines. If the stain bleeds outside the embossing, wipe with a Q-tip or tissue.
- To get inside little areas, squeeze some paint on the design and spread it into the corners with a toothpick.
- The paint tends to puddle up, so lay the painted piece flat until it dries. Weighting down the transparency on the corners will help if necessary.
- Drying time is about 3-4 hours.

HOT TIP

Stained glass paints aren't limited to the transparency paper. Use this same technique on glossy or coated papers, plastic boxes.

▲ Foiling instead of embossing:
- Stamp on the acetate with a permanent or fabric ink.
- Let dry.
- Using the foil adhesive with the super fine tip, follow the outlines of the stamped image.
- Let dry again.
- Now color in with Zig markers, stained glass paints, or fabric markers.

▲ Use Stamp-A-Foil by Enchanted Creations:
- Stamp the image using Stamp-A-Foil Detail, for line-image stamps, directly on the stamp.
- Let dry.
- Foil.
- Color in with fabric markers or the Zig Transparency Pens.

Ideas for mounting your stained glass:

▲ Using a three-panel card,
- Cut a frame in the middle panel. Make it a square, rectangle, heart, oval, etc.
- Mount the transparency on the back side of the frame with double-stick tape.
- Looking at the card from the back, fold over the panel to the *left* onto the middle panel. The acetate will now be sandwiched between the two layers.
- Tape down the left-hand panel to the middle.
- Fold over right-hand side for the back panel of your card.

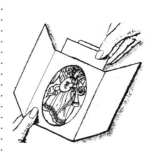

▲ Using a regular folded note card,
- Cut a frame out of the front. Tape down the acetate on the back.
- Line the back with a card just slightly smaller than the first. Tape to the back of the front of the card.

▲ Using two separate pieces of cardstock,
- Cut a matching frame from the center of each card
- With double-stick tape, sandwich the designed acetate between the two.

HOT TIPS

Try black cardstock for the frame. This is very dramatic, and really shows off the stained glass.

Bookmarks:
- *Using a long, narrow design, stamp and color the acetate.*
- *Cut a frame out of two bookmarks.*
- *Sandwich the acetate between the two, and secure with double-stick tape.*

Paper Cutting

You will find true deckle edges on handmade paper. This is the natural finish left by the frame that the paper was made on. You can also create this same look on other papers with some easy techniques.

DECKLING

A deckle edge can reveal the quality of fine paper. It will show off the fibers of the paper, and can add visual emphasis to a design. The deckled edge also blends nicely when you are layering sheets of paper on top of each other.

WET PAPER TEARING

Wet paper tearing is a technique used to create a deckle edge. It offers you a simple way to get a beautiful edge to your papers when you need it. It employs little more than water and a straight-edge ruler, and will give you an elegant, uneven edge, much like a true deckle edge. (Will work on almost all papers, except coated stock.)

▲ Decide where you want your edge, or edges. Mark lightly with a pencil.

For a controlled, torn, feathered edge, use a brush and
- tap water to saturate a line on the paper where you want it to tear.

Allow it to soak until paper is transparent.
- Even thick fibers will usually separate if they are
- thoroughly saturated.

Keeping the paper on a flat surface, carefully and
- gently, but firmly, PULL the paper apart. The fibers of the paper should separate, not tear.

Or,

▲ Take the entire edge of the paper that is to be torn
- away and dip in water.

Use a straight edge if you need to make a straight line,
- while pulling the paper. (Tear as above.)

You can dip the corners in water and tear, to make
- rounded corners, etc.

HOT TIP

Using a long, flat, bottomed container such as Rubbermaid, fill with water just to the height of the edge to be torn away. Dip paper down so it sits across the bottom of the container. When you pull the paper out, you will have a straight edge to tear away.

▲ ▲ ▲

Various cutting tools may be used to cut paper. Use these to make a straight cut, or give it an unusual edge, much like the deckled edge:

CUTTING TOOLS

Scissors. Scissors are useful for small cutting projects.
- ▲ Different types of scissors:
  - For most cutting purposes use a regular-sized scissors.
  - Where you need to get into small areas, a small scissors might work better for you.
  - I have become accustomed to a new concept of scissors by Fiskars. It has a rubberized handle, without the finger hole of most scissors. My hands do not get as cramped, especially if I am doing a lot of cutting.
- ▲ Decorative-edged scissors for special effects. These include:
  - Wavy, scalloped, zipper, alligator edges.
  - Deckle-edged scissors, for a deckle look to paper.
  - Pinking shears.

HOT TIP

To minimize waviness when cutting, move the paper into the scissors while holding the scissor hand still.

Paper cutter. Ideal for most of your straight edge paper and cardboard cutting.
- ▲ For your large, basic cutter, invest in one at least 12" long. My personal favorite is a paper cutter by *Fiskars*, a light-weight, 12" paper cutter with interchangeable blades.. It comes with a straight-edge blade for basic cutting. You can

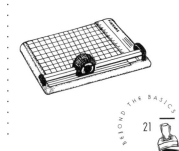

also buy a wave blade, a pinking blade, a deckle-edge blade, and a perforator (*see Postoids* for more on this use). For cutting large sheets of paper with a decorative edge, this is by far the best way to get a straight, even cut.

▲ A little, personal paper cutter, 4"x 6", is a wonderful tool to keep by your side as you work. Use when making small trims, or when cutting paper for layering.

▲ The deckle cutter, imported from Germany, was designed for making the deckled, scalloped edges on the old black and white photos. This is a great cutter for getting a perfectly aligned deckle cut; however, it is very expensive. The Fiskars cutter with the deckle-edge blade will now do the same job.

Mat knife, X-Acto, or single-edged razor. Use for many types of cutting projects. Excellent for cutting into small spaces, and for cutting out only the middle of a piece of paper.

▲ Do your cutting on a flat surface, using either a self-healing cutting mat, or a heavy piece of cardboard under your work.

▲ Be sure the blade of the knife is sharp. A dull blade makes cutting harder, and gives uneven edges.

▲ If cutting straight lines, use a metal-edged ruler to guide the blade for accurate straight edges, cutting from top to bottom.

▲ With your cutting tool, make as many passes as necessary to get through your paper.

HOT TIP

To cut through foam core board, there is a special foam core cutter. It is an X-Acto blade in a special handle that makes cutting through the board easy.

Corner Rounder. A corner rounder is a small, heavy-duty trimmer and does exactly what its name implies: rounds corners. You can use it on photographs, gift cards, postcards, etc., although this is another relatively expensive "toy." And we all know how we love our little toys!

▲ ▲ ▲

The types of stamp inks are dye-based, pigment, permanent and fabric.

▲ ▲ ▲

Inks

Dye-Based Inks

Dye-based inks are water-based, and washable, however permanent once stamped on papers. Use them on all types of papers, other than the oil-based or plastic paper. (See *Papers*.)

Advantages:
- Stamps well.
- Dries quickly.
- Will dry on coated papers.

Disadvantages:
- Will fade with time.
- Hard to use for embossing because it dries so fast.
- Tends to bleed and fuzz on very absorbent papers.

Re-inking the Pads. Simply squeeze ink onto the pad, and allow it to soak in. Better to re-ink several times until you get the right absorbency, than to over-ink the pad.

▲ ▲ ▲

Pigment Inks

Pigment ink (under names such as Inkwell, Niji, Colorbox) is different from normal dye inks; they are thicker, richer and highly fade-resistant. The pigment inks are very bright, vivid, and work great on matte papers, or embossed on any paper. These inks will not fade when embossed, and therefore are perfect for a piece that is going to be on display under lights.

Pigment inks are generally found on foam pads that are raised above the surface of the container, like a sponge. This allows

even a small stamp pad to work with large stamps. Turn a large stamp upside down, and stamp the pad onto the stamp itself until the entire rubber is inked. This is also ideal to ink just a part of an image.

Advantages:
- Resists fading.
- Slow drying time makes it ideal for embossing.
- Colors don't bleed in rainbow pads.
- Can find brilliant colors in these inks.

Disadvantages:
- Must emboss if stamping on coated papers.
- Because it is slow drying, inks can smudge while wet.

Re-inking Pigment Pads. When the ink becomes dry on your pigment pads, it is very simple to re-ink the pad.

▲ With a single-color pad:
- Squeeze a bead of ink zig-zagged on the pad, about 3-5 strips.
- Use a flat tool, such as a craft or popsickle stick, or dull knife, to spread the ink back and forth on the sponge pad.
- Gently push down as you spread.
- The ink will work itself into the pad within a few seconds.

▲ For the 3-,5-, and 12-color pads, use the same techniques, one color at a time. The only difference is that each area you are working with will be smaller.

▲ ▲ ▲

Rainbow Pads

Rainbow stamp pads are the ones that have more than one color on the pad. They are found in both dye and pigment ink pads.

Stamp Francisco makes the Abracadada pads, a beautiful hand-colored, dye-based rainbow ink pad. Other companies also have some beautiful lines of hand-colored rainbow pads available. (Companies such as RubberBabyBuggyBumplers, Alice In Rubberland and NameBrands.)

To keep the pads looking and working their best for a long time:

▲ Store the dye-based pads upside down, so the ink remains on top.

TAKE NOTE

Do not store the dye-based raibow pads on their sides. The colors will run down and bleed together. Keep your non-pigment rainbow pads flat, and upside down.

▲ To help retard the blending of colors, you can keep these pads in the refrigerator.
▲ Use them regularly or they will blend and turn murky. These pads benefit from a lot of use.
▲ To stamp on a rainbow pad, tap the stamp on the pad. Lift the stamp and move it just slightly on the pad and stamp again. This will help blend the colors on the stamp and you won't get definite color lines when stamped.
▲ Pigment-based rainbow pads should be stored right side up. The colors do not bleed into each other as they do in the dye ones.

HOT TIP

Move the stamp slightly in the direction of the darker end of the pad. You don't want to contaminate the pad by stamping from the darker colors onto the lighter colors of the pad.

You can make your own dye or pigment ink stamp pads. This is a great way to get some unusual combinations.

▲ Different stamp pads you can use:
- Buy blank pads, either the flat felt pads or the raised sponge-type pads.
- Or use a double thickness of white felt you buy in a craft or fabric store.

▲ Use re-inkers of either the dye paint or the pigment paint and combine colors you want.

▲ Make dots or other shapes on the pad, for unusual inkings.

▲ Use these pads, or a sheet of glass or plastic, or a plasticized foam meat tray, to also brush out goache, fabric ink, calligraphy inks or other water soluble paint .

▲ ▲ ▲

Permanent Inks

Permanent inks can be either water-soluble or solvent-based. The water-soluble ink can be used on all papers, and other surfaces as well.

Permanent inks that are solvent-based dry by evaporation rather than absorption. These work well on all but oil-based papers. They will not fade with time or light. Clean your stamps well immediately after using with a solvent cleaner. These inks can be used on surfaces other than paper, such as wood, glass, plastic, cellophane, foil, etc.

HOT

TIP

Stamping on these non-porous surfaces is different than stamping on paper. Hold your stamp straight and lightly 'kiss' the surface.

To use permanent inks on paper, be sure to ink the stamp well before stamping. Stamp immediately, as permanent inks dry fast.

The advantages to permanent inks:
- Dries fast.
- Can color immediately.
- Does not run, bleed or fade.
- Can stamp on all types of paper.

▲ ▲ ▲

Fabric Inks

Stamping on fabric with fabric inks:
▲ Spread a thin layer of the paint on a piece of plexiglass, styrofoam plates, or disposable pie tins.
▲ Stamp directly into the paint, or use a small sponge brush to brush the paint on the stamp.
▲ Or, make up your own pad with a double thickness of white felt.
  - Pour a little of the fabric paint on the felt, spread it out with a knife or spatula.
  - Work the paint into the felt so none of it pools on the surface.
  - Next, press the rubber stamp onto the felt.

▲ Check the rubber surface to see that the paint is evenly distributed. The paint should not be too thick (leaves puddles of paint on the stamp instead of thinly coating it), nor too thin (stamp not evenly covered).
▲ Nice, big graphic stamps make great images on fabrics.
▲ When using these solid rubber stamps, you will often get an uneven color when stamped.
▲ To avoid a lot of this blotchy look you get with the solid rubber, wait a minute or so before stamping the design on your fabric. It takes this time for the paint to "even out". The ink won't dry on the stamp in this amount of time.

HOT TIP

A quick fix for any blotchy image you get: Fill in the design with a small brush or a Q-tip, using the same fabric color you stamped with.

HOT TIP

Fabric paint can be cleaned off easily. Hold the stamp under running water. Using an old toothbrush or nailbrush, give it a little scrubbing to get any paint out of the crevices.

▲ Use fabric glitter and puff paint to enhance your stamped designs.

▲ Designs with line image drawings can be stamped with a dark color, such as black. Then color in with fabric pens.

▲ Another method for line images is *paper transfer*.

- Stamp your design on paper using pigment ink.
- Any paper that you emboss on can then be turned over and ironed onto fabric. You do not need special transfer paper. Vellum paper works especially well with this technique.
- Use clear embossing powder and emboss the image.
- After it's been embossed on paper, turn it over and iron on to the fabric.
- The image is clearer, brighter and proved to be more washable.
- You can stamp out your whole design first. Then place it on your fabric exactly as you want it. This gives you the freedom to visually place and replace for design and balance.

Step 1a: Embossing

To emboss an image, stamp your design on paper using a *very wet ink*, pour embossing powder over the image and tap off excess powder. (Be sure to save.) With a heating element, heat the powder until it melts, giving a raised effect.

▲ ▲ ▲

The first consideration in embossing is not the paper. If the right inks are used, you can emboss on virtually any surface: glossy paper, matte paper, oil-based paper, recycled paper, wood, plastics, acetates, fabric.

The ink needs to stay wet long enough to hold the embossing powder.

For colored inks, *pigment inks* are the perfect medium.

Clear embossing ink, another way to stamp a wet image on the paper, is colorless (or slightly tinted). It comes in either a roll-on bottle and the ink is dabbed onto the stamp; or a pad that is inked with embossing fluid, so you stamp on the pad, then on the paper.

The Ink

HOT TIP

To avoid an over-juicy image when using the roller applicator. Pat the inked stamp lightly on a scrap paper first, then stamp on your paper. In this way, excess ink will absorb on the scrap paper, giving you a clean image to emboss.

Since these inks are virtually colorless, use them only when you are embossing with an opaque, colored embossing powder. If you using clear embossing powder over embossing ink, the image will rise, but be transparent.

Make your own clear embossing pads. Use embossing liquids, available from various stamp companies, and a blank pad. Ink up the pad with the ink in the bottle, which is enough for many re-applications.

Glycerin, purchased in drug and craft stores, can be used as embossing ink, since embossing ink is made with glycerin. It is a thick liquid that needs to be mixed with 2-3 parts water. Pour into a sponge-top applicator (like those used for postage stamps), or apply it to a blank foam pad. The mixture can also be applied to the rubber of the stamp with a make-up type sponge, or painted on with a small paintbrush.

HOT TIP

Dilute the glycerin 50-50 with water and put it into a spray bottle. You can then spray your entire card or envelope and emboss the whole thing. Or mask off the parts you don't want embossed before spraying.

Markers, by themselves, do not stay wet long enough to emboss. For solid-rubber images you want to color with markers and emboss:

▲ Stamp on the glycerine or embossing pad first, then color the stamp with markers. This keeps the marker ink wetter longer, so you can emboss the colored image with a clear powder.

▲ Or the opposite: color the stamp with the markers, then stamp the colored image directly on the embossing ink pad. Stamp onto the paper. You will end up with color on the "clear" embossing ink pad, but it should not affect further stampings. You can always wash the foam pads under running water, and re-ink.

Embossing Pens. There are different types of pens on the market that can be used to emboss writing, printing, flour-ishes, borders, etc. An "erasable" ballpoint pen will work, as well as ones with different tips. There is a pen with a chiseled point for calligraphic writing; and an embossing pen from Ranger Ink whose tip is like a Marvy brush marker, but it's filled with clear embossing liquid.

Embossing edges of your cards (this works on torn edges as well):

▲ Use a glue stick or an embossing pen, or an embossing edger (a small squeeze bottle with embossing ink) on the edges. Dip in embossing powder and heat.

▲ For perfectly straight embossed edges, apply a row of double stick tape around the perimeter of your work. Dip in embossing powder (this also works by dipping in loose glitter). Tap off the excess powder, and heat.

HOT TIPS

Tips, Tricks and Techniques *with embossing inks:*

• To double emboss, color in a design already embossed on your paper. Then brush the colored image with clear embossing ink and emboss with clear powder.

• For embossing an entire area of an already stamped image, use a reverse mask, then brayer embossing fluid over the exposed design.

• To emboss with an over-sized stamp, put clear embossing ink on a makeup sponge and dab it evenly across the large stamp.

Over-embossing:

▲ For a glassy finish on a card, or to give a look of lacquer, especially nice on stamped jewelry, try a special technique I call over-embossing:

• Sprinkle clear embossing powder over the piece.

• Heat from underneath until all powder has melted.

• Continue to sprinkle and heat until you have built up a clear, smooth, shiny surface that looks like lacquer.

The Powder

Embossing powder is the second ingredient needed to emboss. It is essentially a lithographic powder used by printers to give printing an embossed, raised image.

Embossing powders are either transparent, semi-transparent, or opaque. With opaque powders—such as silver, gold, copper, bronze—the powder will cover the embossing ink completely, and the ink will not show through. You can use any colored pigment ink, or a clear embossing ink. The image you get will be the color of the embossing powder. (Sometimes black pigment ink will turn the embossing powder a slightly darker color.)

With transparent, or semi-transparent powders, the color of the ink under the powder will show through after embossing. So, the color of ink you use is as important as the color of powder. Included in this category are powders such as clear, pearl, sparkle, and most colored sparkle powders.

TAKE

NOTE

Caution: Be sure to shake any bottle of embossing powder with glitter as the glitter in the powder stays on the surface. When the embossing powder contains too much glitter, often the integrity of the embossing powder is lost and the result is that much of the design does not emboss. Test these powders first. You can always add some clear powder.

HOT

TIP

To make embossing really easy, buy 2 or more bottles of the same color embossing powder at one time, and pour them in square Rubbermaid® sandwich containers. You can dip the card in, scoop up the powder on the paper, and tap excess back into the container. Keep a plastic spoon in the container to scoop onto paper too large to dip. No mess, no loss of powder.

Tips, Tricks and Techniques *using powders:*

- Psychedelic embossing powder is a fun, novelty powder. As you heat it, the powder changes color. When heating, first heat the entire design to the first color of blue/purple. This takes a light touch. Then direct your heat source to the areas you wish to change to additional colors.
- Psychedelic powder is great over black ink and also on black paper over silver or gold pigment ink.
- Mix bronze and a little black embossing powder together. Over black ink it will give a mottled, aged look, like an old coin.
- Vertigris is a green and black powder that looks great with greenery and architectural designs. Another embossing powder is Terracotta. This has the color and texture of clay pots. Both are manufactured by Ranger Industries and sold through various stamp companies, such as Delafield.
- Experiment. Check out the new combinations coming along all the time.

▲ ▲ ▲

A final element in embossing: a heat source. I love to emboss because embossing makes my images sharper, and has a permanency to it. When embossed, the image will not fade under lights, or over time.

If you find you like to emboss, a heat gun is a necessity! But I'm not sure which comes first. Until I discovered the heat gun, I felt that getting my iron ready, or the stove burner heated, prohibited me from embossing very often. Especially if I just wanted to emboss one or two images. Then I discovered the heat gun, and life has never been the same! So...you like to emboss, and therefore you might buy a heat gun; or you might

Heat Sources

buy a heat gun, and discover you love to emboss.

Heat is needed to make the embossing powder rise on the stamped image. A heat source can be the electric burner on the stove, a toaster, iron, light bulb, mug warmer or heat gun.

To emboss:
For all heat sources, except the heat gun:
▲ Hold your paper, image side up, over the heat source. The heat will come from underneath.
▲ Heat until the powder melts. Depending on the heat source and the size of the image, it can take approximately 10-30 seconds.
▲ Be sure the entire image has been heated sufficiently and all the powder has melted.
▲ If the paper you are using is too dense, you may want to hold it, image-side down, over the heat.

With a heat tool:
▲ Leave your paper right side up on your table.
▲ Turn on your heat gun, and heat from the *top* of your paper.
▲ Because you are heating from above, the heat tool works well for embossing other surfaces as well. It will emboss on wood, plastic, fabric, etc.

HOT TIPS

Turn the heat gun on, hold it away from the image for a few seconds. It needs a moment to get hot enough. A cold heat gun, for example, can blow away much of the glitter in a glitter embossing powder before it begins to melt the powder.

If you've ever wondered how long you have from the time you put the embossing powder on the wet pigment ink, until the time you heat it: don't worry. The powder will

stick to the ink until you heat it...I have waited a day before heating, and could probably wait longer. You certainly have enough time to put powder on many cards before heating them all at once.

When putting embossing powder on the stamped image, powder will often stick to other parts of the paper as well. This is because of fingerprint oils and static electricity.

▲ Pour embossing powder on the paper and tap off as much of the excess that is able to slide off on its own.

▲ Turn the paper over. Flick your finger on the back of the card. Flicking the back will help to encourage any stray powder to fly off.

▲ If powder remains, use a very small, fine sable brush to brush away excess powder very carefully.

▲ If you are having a lot of trouble embossing because static makes the embossing powder cling to everything, try a fabric softener sheet. Wipe the surface with the sheet before stamping and putting the embossing powder on.

HOT TIPS

Tips, Tricks and Techniques:

• *The weather is a big factor in embossing success. In very humid weather you will have a hard time getting the embossing powder to stick. Under these conditions, be sure you use a fresh, wet pigment ink pad, or embossing pad.*

• *For a color on color look, emboss with the same color as your paper. For example, use black pigment ink on black paper and emboss with clear powder. Or white powder on white paper, etc. This makes for a very subtle, sophisticated look.*

• *For rainbow embossing:*
  • *Stamp a long design.*
  • *Sprinkle your first color on the first portion of the design. Tap off.*
  • *Sprinkle another color next to it, on a portion*

HOT

TIPS

of the design. Tap off.

- *Continue with as many colors as desired. For example, sprinkle gold, silver, copper.*
- *Each new color will not stick where there is already powder. Be careful not to get it on fresh ink you don't want covered.*

▲ ▲ ▲

Making Your Own Powder Combinations

You can take embossing powder and add very, very fine loose glitter to make your own sparkle embossing powder. The heavier glitters will not work, as they will melt when heated. Also, be aware that too much glitter will prevent there being enough embossing powder to adhere to the image, and will not emboss well.

▲ ▲ ▲

Dry Embossing and Stenciling

When talking about embossing, there is often confusion between the embossing done with rubber stamps and embossing powders, and a technique called "dry embossing." Also known as "paper embossing," the entire design is raised, giving a raised paper image...very simple, but so elegant.

The elements of dry embossing include a stencil, an embossing tool and a light source. The stencils can be brass, plastic or even cardboard; the embossing tool has a wood or plastic handle, and a metal ball on each end, called a burnisher; the light source can be a light box, a flashlight or bulb under glass, or a window (used in daylight).

To emboss:
1. Tape the stencil to the right side of your paper with masking or lift-off tape.
2. Turn the paper over, and tape it to the light source (either on top of a light box, or onto a window). This will help to hold it steady.

3. "Supple," textured papers work best. The most effective papers are those with some cotton content. They're softer and bend rather than crack. I also emboss on glossy coated paper with no problem, and it looks great.
4. On the reverse, start by gently moving the burnisher along the edge of the design. Once the shape is visible, use a bit more pressure, and continue. You only need to outline the design by running around the edge of the stencil...the rest of the design will "pop out."
   CAUTION: pressing too hard may tear the paper.
5. When you're done, flip the paper over. Loosen one piece of tape. Does it look the way you want it to look? If so, remove the other piece of tape. If not, refasten tape and work as needed.

USING A WINDOW

After you have embossed, your design is a raised image on your paper. Leave it as it is for an elegant look, or add color. You can use pigment inks applied with sponges, oil or wax crayons, chalks, colored glitter. You can even emboss with clear embossing powder over your color image.

USING A LIGHTBOX

▲ ▲ ▲

Leave the stencil on the paper. This keeps the color on the raised part and helps to keep color from bleeding onto the rest of the paper.

ADDING COLOR

Pigment Ink
▲ Take a small round stencil brush, sponge or Q-Tip. Dip on a pigment ink pad, then swirl on scrap paper first, to prevent too much ink on the brush.
▲ Place brush or sponge on stencil, and move towards the paper. You will be working from the edge to the center of the design.
▲ Color with whatever colors you choose. You can shade and highlight with 2 or more colors of the same tint.

Watercolors

- ▲ Use pale, soft colors applied lightly.
- ▲ Dab frequently to absorb the wetness, or your paper will curl.
- ▲ Using a wet brush on pigment ink pads can also work as watercolors.

Oil Crayons

- ▲ You need a crayon, paper towels, wax paper and a stencil brush.
- ▲ With the paper towel, wipe some of the wax off the crayon.
- ▲ Scribble plenty of the crayon on the wax paper.
- ▲ Use a stencil brush and daub it in the paint until you have a respectable amount in the bristles.
- ▲ With an up and down motion, color the paper...with the stencil still taped in place.
- ▲ Continue in this manner until you achieve the look you want.

Soft chalks

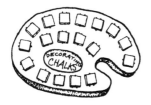

- ▲ Sof-T Chalks by Craft-T Products, can be used to color the embossed designs. The chalks come on a palette with 25 "compacts" of colors.
- ▲ Use a sponge to apply color.

Embossing

After coloring you can emboss, if you wish.

- ▲ Leave the stencil in place.
- ▲ Brush the colored, raised image with embossing ink.
- ▲ Put on clear, pearl or sparkle embossing powder.
- ▲ Heat for an "embossed, embossed" image.

Glitter

Rather than coloring, for a more delicate look you can use colored glitter.

- ▲ Apply glue with a glue stick.

▲ Sprinkle on very, very fine colored glitter.
When you are finished, remove the tape and take off the
stencil.

▲ ▲ ▲

Plastic stencils

There are plastic stencils as well as brass ones. These are
meant for wall stencilling, but they can be used on paper as
well.

H O T

T I P

*White plastic stencils can be hard to see when you're
embossing. To get the design to show through your paper,
take the plastic stencil and run a black felt-tip marker
around the rim of the design. (Be sure to mark on the side
that will not be touching the paper.) Let dry.*

Combine your stamping with both dry paper embossing and
stenciling. Use either the embossing/stenciling or the stamping as an accent to the other. An equal amount of both tends to
make neither technique very interesting.

The following are some suggestions for combining the two, but
experiment, and you'll come up with some of your own ideas.

▲ Use the stencil or dry-embossed design as a border for a
rubber stamped design on a card.

▲ Stencil in elements of your design, such as clouds, waves,
stars in a sky. It adds a twist to a normally all-stamped
card. (See *Scenery* in the color photo section.)

Step 2: Coloring the Image

Markers

Colored markers are probably the most basic coloring technique for stamps. Markers can be used on almost all papers, except those papers with an oil-based coating.

Look for water-based markers that have bright, transparent color. Some of the less expensive markers, especially, have very opaque colors. The lines in the design of the image will be obliterated if the ink is not transparent enough.

Some of the best markers for use with stamps are:
▲ Marvy Markers, by Marvy-Uchida
▲ Tombow Markers
▲ Staedtler Markers
▲ Pigma's Sumi Brush Markers (These are more expensive than the others, but their advantage is they will not fade with time.)

All of the above markers are well worth your investment, and come in a wide variety of colors.

Colored Pencils

Colored pencils are beautiful on all types of rag, recycled and other matte papers, however, not on coated papers.. Experiment to get an idea of the different effects. The quality of the pencils *does* matter. Good quality pencils include ones by Staedtler, Caran d'Ache, Berol Prismacolor, and Derwent.

In working with pencils, lightly lay down one color. Then lay down a complementary color, or an adjacent color on the color wheel (see "Working with Color," in the *Basic Principles*

chapter). Pencils blend easily, and you can get variations and gradations of color through combining.

The waxes and pigments of the pencils do not cover all the tiny raised parts of textured paper. Since the entire surface, therefore, is not completely covered, it is like mixing white with the colors. If you want a pink, use a red. The paper will serve as the white that reduces the red tone.

Pencil colors can be mixed to make other colors. The colors and intensity change by the sequence of adding one color over the other, as dark colors cover light colors more. To get a light green, you would apply a blue, then over-color with yellow. To get dark green, apply the blue over the yellow.

To blend the colors of the pencil, you can burnish over your whole colored design with a white pencil, pressing really hard. The white lightens the tones, blends the lines, and reduces the characteristics of the grain of the paper. You can then go back over the area with one of the original colors, or choose a different color, to bring back an intensity.

A neutral or colorless felt-tip pen can be used with watercolor pencils. They are called "blenders" because they do just as they say: they blend colors.

Colored pencils are also a valuable help in coloring in watercolors. After using watercolors, or wetting your watercolor pencil drawing, go back in with the pencils. You can use it to darken certain areas of the drawing, putting in values, shading and highlights.

▲ ▲ ▲

Watercolors

A soft watercolor look can be achieved in many ways. Water-color will give soft shades of coloring and subtle blending. Be sure to watercolor on non-coated paper (this won't work on glossy paper). Some papers respond better than others, so experiment. Different papers will give different looks. Try textured paper as well as flat surfaced papers.

▲ ▲ ▲

Water-Based Markers

Use *Marvy or Tombow* water-based pens directly on a stamp to achieve a watercolor look.

▲ Color a solid-rubber stamp using the blending technique.
  - Color on the rubber with markers, starting with light colors and graduating to darker ones.
  - Go back and pull the light colors into the dark ones using your markers.
  - Huff on the rubber and stamp on paper.
  - Take a small brush, such as a triple 0 brush, and dip the brush in water. Touch it to the stamped image. The "flat" colors come alive when the water touches them and create an entirely different, watercolor effect.
  - This looks especially nice with floral designs, like a Posh design stamp.

▲ Color an *open, line-type image* with color.
  - For example: a rose stamp with leaves. Apply color to the rose in red, and green to the leaf.
  - Stamp on your card.
  - Use a very fine 000 wet paintbrush to pull the color into the non-colored part of the design from the colored lines.
  - Using a small, plastic watercolor palette, scribble with your Marvy color in the "wells" of a plastic watercolor palette. Then dip a small, wet brush in the color. Use
  - this to watercolor your images after stamping.

▲ ▲ ▲

Watercolor pencils

First, color in your stamped design using watercolor pencils. With a tiny brush and just a bit of water, wash over the colored area. It blends those blank spaces beautifully. You can use your brush to fan out the color as well.

Or, take a wet brush. Run it across the watercolor pencil, and paint in with your "watercolor."

▲ ▲ ▲

Watercolors and Pigment Refill Inks

Try this unusual watercolor technique with simple, large, open-design stamps:

▲ Stamp the design on watercolor paper, or heavy cardstock, using embossing ink.
▲ Sprinkle with metallic embossing powder and heat.
▲ Prepare watercolor paint by diluting with water to a thin, milky consistency. Or use watered-down pigment refill ink.
▲ Take your watercolor paper with the embossed image and hold under the faucet to get the surface completely wet.
▲ Tap off excess water.
▲ Lay flat with the embossed side up.
▲ Using a small paintbrush, dip into the watercolor and lightly dot the color into the open areas of your embossed image.
▲ The colors will flow softly from the brush tip onto the wet surface.
▲ The embossed lines will keep the watercolors inside the image.

▲ ▲ ▲

Pigment Pads

Embellish embossed artwork with a watercolor look using multi-color pigment pads. This is quick and easy, and produces a soft, hand-painted look.

▲ Stamp and emboss your design on cardstock.

▲ Lightly wet a small brush in water.
▲ Apply the wet brush to a color on the pigment pad.
▲ Brush the color on the embossed stamped design.
▲ Try blending colors together.
▲ Repeat these steps with other colors until you have finished your design.

▲ ▲ ▲

Pens

There are some great pens that are handy to have around for special effects in stamping. Because of their varying widths, they also make great backgrounds. Use them for "wallpaper" and for making stripes, plaids, dots, frames, etc.

Posterman Paint Pens

These paint markers by E.K. Success contain waterbased pigment ink. They come in 22 colors, including metallic colors, and can be colored directly on the stamps. The bright colors look especially good on dark paper.

Posterman Pens also come in a white opaque, in four different tip widths. You can use it to write on dark paper and dark envelopes, to add a border around your stamping. Dot it on designs you want to add highlights, or to give the look of snow. With the finer tips, you can make stripes and patterns on dark paper for "wallpaper" backgrounds.

Micron Pens

These come in different widths varying from extra fine to extra, extra fine. These pens can be used for adding backgrounds, or used to make the ground or a shelf to sit something on. They also can be used for writing when a very fine writing point is needed.

Zig Clean Color, and Super Clean Color

The markers have narrow tips, in many bright and deep colors for lining backgrounds and making frames. The water-based pens are also good for coloring on stamps, especially where you need accurate detail. By huffing on the pen-colored stamp, you will be able to get quite a few additional stampings out of one coloring.

Correction Pen

A white-out correction pen in the form of a ball-point can be used to make stripes on dark paper, snow, snowflakes, frame a picture. And it's wonderful for writing on your dark envelopes, especially black.

HOT TIP

Test the pen before using each time, as it has a tendency to clog, then "spit out" a blob of white.

Step 3: Glitter and Other Dimensions

Special effects like glittering, foiling, etc. are the third element of the Basic 1,2,3's of stamping.

▲ ▲ ▲

Adhesives

Zig Two-Way Glue Stick

The glue stick I generally refer to in this book is the *Zig 2-Way Glue Stick*, unless some other glue is mentioned. It is called "2-Way" because it is both a permanent bonding glue, and a temporary, tacky glue. The glue stick is tinted blue, but dries clear. When the glue is wet (blue), it will form a permanent bond. When the glue has been allowed to dry colorless, it will make a temporary bond.

The two-way glue stick is in a barrel applicator, with a chiseled tip. Use its wide part to put down a large area of glue; use the side to apply small points of adhesive. The chiseled tip makes a wonderful calligraphic tip for writing names, and applying embossing powder or glitter.

Dryline Adhesive

Dryline adhesive comes in a handy applicator, and is available in both permanent and temporary adhesive. You pull the applicator along the line or shape you want the adhesive on.

The permanent Dryline adhesive is the same as double-stick tape, however, seems handier since you can roll on the exact amount you need and works well for getting into small areas. The temporary Dryline Adhesive can be used for making masks without using a Post-it® note.

Studio-Tac

Another great adhesive, as a temporary bond for masking, is called *Studio Tac* by Letraset. This is an alternative to messy sprays and adhesives with harmful fumes. Found at art stores, it comes on a tablet with sheets of glue in little bubbles. Rub your mask on the sheet, and a tacky glue adheres to the back of your paper.

PEEL   PRESS

Foam tape

Double-stick *foam tape* (also known as poster tape) adds dimension to your stampings. Simply cut out designs you want 3-d'ed on the paper. Then attach to the paper with the foam tape. You can control the height of the object by using more than one layer of foam tape, if you wish.

For extra height, use *foam insulation tape*. This comes in both white or black, and is about 1/2" high. Or 3D foam dots, available from some stamp companies and art supply stores.

FOAM TAPE

Glue Gun

A *glue gun*, much like foam tape, is used to get dimension. The advantage of the glue gun is the higher depth you can get. The height is controllable by the amount of hot glue you pile on. This works well for Paper Toling (see *Paper Toling*.)

Sloman's Quick Glue

This is a great glue for special situations. It is a glue made for gluing porous surfaces to non-porous surfaces. Use it to apply postage stamps to designed envelopes that have a finish that repels the stamps, such as glossy paper, or an all-embossed envelope. Also good for adhering stamps or labels to magazine pages, or gluing sequins to paper. It also works for putting plastic to paper, plastic to wood, etc.

Yes Paste

Yes brand paste is an acid-free, vegetable paste for permanent creations. A very thick paste that comes in a wide-mouth jar, it tends to get thicker and harder after it's opened and used. This is a wonderful glue to use with very thin papers, such as Oriental papers, and great in book-making projects. However, because of its drying tendency, it is hard to work with after a few uses.

HOT TIP

To combat the hardening, apply water to the paste using a spray bottle of water. Spray the paste with the water, and mix. Also, spray the paste with a thin film of water before closing the jar after use. This may retard the hardening somewhat.

▲ ▲ ▲

Glitter Writing Glue

This is a specially-formulated glue available from The Art Institute and Enchanted Creations, that, when dry, remains high and three-dimensional. It is meant for super-fine glitter. Once the glitter is put on the adhesive, it will not flake off.

Use this for "glitter writing," a technique of using the adhesive for writing or making accents on your cards. Sprinkle the glitter over the glue for a truly glitzy look. It is fun to sprinkle different colors much like "rainbow embossing."

▲ ▲ ▲

Paper Tole

Paper tole is a unique way of adding dimension to designs. Using either silicon gel, bought in hardware stores, or hot glue, this technique really lifts the images off the page. The curvature of the paper hides the glue.

Look for designs that have large individual elements. A large floral design with big petals and leaves, for example, lends itself well to this technique. Each leaf will be cut out separately and reapplied with the adherent.

To get this look:

1. Stamp the image on your base card, and again on a separate piece of cardstock.
2. Color the images on both papers exactly the same.
3. Cut out the individual pieces on the extra cardstock. (If the design is a flower cut along the petal lines only to the flower center, being careful to not cut off the petals. Use your judgement, as there are some flowers that will work with each petal cut individually.)
4. Lay each piece flat on your palm, right side down. Keep your palm flat, not curved.
5. Take the back side of a spoon and rub over the back of the image in all directions so it will curve up. Or, curl each piece around a pencil lightly to give it a curve.
6. Apply a generous amount of clear silicone sealant to the underside of the cut-out petal. Make it as high as you want the image to raise; the curvature of the design will hide the sealant.
7. Holding by an edge, place each piece directly over the exact image on your original card. Use a toothpick or tweezers to position it just right.
8. Allow to dry.

TAKE ✋ **NOTE**

Try to avoid getting the sealant on your fingers. If you do, wipe it off quickly. Don't try to rub it off as you would rubber cement ... it will get all over you!

▲ ▲ ▲

Spray fixative

A spray fixative is used to protect stamped cards. This is especially useful when sending cards and stamped envelopes through the mail. Use the matte finish for a non-finish. The glossy finishes will add shine to the design.

Sprays

Most of the spray fixatives suitable for pastels will work, but it's best to try a sample first. Two brands I have found that work well are Krylon and Blair.

TAKE

NOTE

Caution: the spray may tend to yellow your colors and darken them. If you spray too close to the paper, the inks tend to run. Follow the directions on the can, and try a small section first.

Spray Mount

High tack spray glues can be used with both glitter or embossing powder to glitter or emboss a large area. If you don't wish to spray the entire card or envelope, make a mask to cover up that part or parts of the piece you do not want covered. Sprinkle ultra fine glitter over the glue, or sprinkle on embossing powder and heat.

This can also be used to adhere paper to paper. This works in making collages, mounting your work to cardstock, etc. Spray mounts come in both permanent and temporary adhesive.

Spray Glitter

This is something like non-sticky hairspray with fine glitter in an aerosol can. Spray this on your piece, again masking off anything you don't want glittered. When dry, you have a glittery finish.

TAKE

NOTE

CAUTION: Make sure you do any spraying in a very well-ventilated room. Spraying outdoors is ideal.

New Dimensions

A three-dimensional, "fuzzy" finish can be added to designs with a soft, velvety flocking material. It comes in many colors, dry and loose, in small bottles. Use it to flock teddy bears and animals, add sand, etc.

Flocking

▲ Apply a layer of glue to the design you want flocked. Let the glue get tacky.
▲ Types of glue that work:
  • Aleene's Tacky Glue
  • Elmer's Glue
  • Glue Stick
  • Liquid Applique or Puff-It

▲ Over the glue, sprinkle on the flock and pat down.
  • The adhesive must remain wet long enough for firm anchorage of the flock.
  • To get a thin layer of flocking that lets you see the stamped image beneath, apply the glue very lightly.
  • With a heavier layer of glue, the flock is thicker and hides the image.
  • Keep in mind that when using heavier flocking, everything underneath will be obscured.

▲ A small amount of flocking will go a long way.
  If you have trouble getting into very fine places, sequin glues in small accordian bottles from craft stores will work. It allows you to get into tiny areas, it's easy to outline around the stamped image, and will not pick up the color of the ink or colored design.
▲ Let the flock set overnight. In the morning flick and shake off the loose flocking and pour the excess back in the bottle.

▲ ▲ ▲

Foils

Foils will enhance your stamped images. There are different types of foils and adhesives on the market.

One type of foil uses either a brush-on adhesive that comes in a bottle, much like nail polish, or a squeeze bottle with a very fine tip. The brush-on adhesive will cover larger parts of a design. The fine-tipped applicator is used to write with or to outline a design. A glue stick can also be used with these foils.

▲ Make your stamped impression.

▲ Apply the foil adhesive sparingly to the area you would like to dress up.

▲ Let it dry completely. This is very important. With the adhesives, you can't let it dry too long. Overnight drying will not hurt the process. You can shorten the drying time by using a hair dryer or heat gun.

▲ Lay the foil on the tacky adhesive. Press the dull side of the foil lightly to the adhesve.

▲ Rub with your finger or with a smooth instrument, such as a burnisher or back of a spoon.

▲ Lift the foil from the adhesive. It leaves an embossed foil appearance.

TAKE

NOTE

CAUTION: The foil will stick to an embossed image, so be careful not lay foil on any part of an embossed design you do not want foiled.

Problem:
Your foil isn't sticking to the adhesive.
Solution:
The glue may not have dried enough. The glue must dry to a tacky finish. The time it takes can vary. The weather and humidity can affect the time.

Problem:
Foiled image remains tacky.
Solution:
▲ Dust lightly with corn starch or baby talc to reduce sticking to other items, or...
▲ Try rubbing canning wax over the foiled image, or...
▲ Sprinkle glitter over the foiled design.

HOT TIP

To foil edges neatly and straight, use double-stick tape. Place a piece of double-stick tape at the edge of your card (cut it the width you want the foil line). Press the foil onto it. It works for even lines and you don't have to wait for it to dry.

Foiltiques, by Enchanted Creations, has 2 different types of glue that are applied directly on the stamp for using with foils. Stamp-It Detail is for fine-line stamps; the other, for solid rubber image stamps, is called Stamp-It-Bold.

For using Stamp-It Detail on fine-line images:
1. Brush a layer of adhesive onto a plastic or styrofoam plate.
2. Press your rubber stamp on the adhesive as you would into an ink pad.
3. Stamp onto your paper. Be careful not to rock your stamp.
4. Let dry, about 3-6 minutes.

HOT TIP

While waiting for the adhesive to dry on the paper, clean your stamp. You want to clean the adhesive off immediately, unless you plan to stamp with the adhesive again right away. The water-based adhesive will clean with soap and water. Use a toothbrush to get into the crevices of the rubber. If you let the adhesive sit on the stamp too long, soak with solvent stamp cleaner, or rubbing alcohol, for about 5 minutes.

5. Select the color foil or foils you want to use.

6. Press the dull side of the foil onto the adhesive.
7. Rub with your finger, or a foil tool.
8. Lift off the foil carrier.

HOT TIP

If the foil did not adhere in some areas, go back and press foil on the missing area.
If foil adhesive seems to be missing in an area, add adhesive, wait until dry, then re-foil that area.

Use Stamp-It Bold for the solid-rubber, silhouette type stamps:

1. Brush a medium layer of adhesive directly on the stamp. Use a brush 1/4" wide. (A thinner brush will leave brush strokes.)
2. Or, put some adhesive on a styrofoam plate, and stamp as you would on an ink pad.
3. Stamp the image. Do not rock the stamp. Press the stamp firmly down on the paper, then lift straight off. (Do not lift at an angle, as you will drag the adhesive and get a blurry image.)
4. It should dry in about 3 minutes or less. Follow the instructions above for cleaning your stamp.
5. Press the foil to the adhesive design, shiny side up.
6. Rub the foil with your fingernail or burnisher until you can see that the foil has lifted off the foil carrier.
7. Remove the carrier, and your foiled design is complete.

▲ ▲ ▲

Liquid Applique

Another product that gives a three-dimensional effect to your work is Liquid Applique. Originally made for fabric, it works on paper as well, and adds another dimension to rubber stamping. It will puff up on the paper after heating, and makes wonderful snow, little puffy flowers, icing on a cake, etc.

Liquid Applique is made by Marvy-Uchida, and comes in squeezable tubes. Another product much like Liquid Applique is *Puff-It*, from Enchanted Creations. Both products act alike and have basically the same properties. Puff-It also comes in a thinner consistency for use in an airbrush.

Since both Liquid Applique and Puff-It act alike, unless otherwise noted, all instructions work for both.
▲ Apply very sparingly on your design.
▲ Liquid Applique can be heated immediately, although it is best left to set overnight before heating. Can be heated with a heat gun, or, unlike embossing powder, also with a hair dryer.
▲ Heat from underneath the paper for less heat. It puffs up almost instantly.
▲ Liquid Applique and Puff-It come in many colors. Try the brown and black for spooky Halloween effects and for creepy, crawly creatures. Use dots of the pastels to simulate a field of flowers. Experiment for other looks.

Color can be added to white Liquid Applique.
▲ Wet Liquid Applique will often inadvertently pick up the color under it.

HOT

TIP

To help prevent this, wait until the inks are dry before applying. This will help a bit, but you will often get some color regardless of what you do.

▲ To add color deliberately, use a pallet of pigment ink refills, watered down to a thin ink.
▲ Spray the puffed image with a mister to dampen design.
▲ Dab off *excess* water with paper towel.
▲ Dip small paintbrush into diluted ink and pat onto wet design. The colors will flow because the casting is damp.
▲ The softer colorings look best with this technique.

Glitter can be added to Liquid Applique.

▲ Liquid Applique has a "rubbery" texture that allows the glitter to stick. Glitter can be added at any time...even days later!

▲ Add glitter while Liquid Applique is still wet.

▲ You can also sprinkle colored and opalescent embossing powders on the Liquid Applique.

- The color of the embossing powder will be the dominant color.
- Add the powder over any color Liquid Applique.
- Try different combinations for different effects.

▲ ▲ ▲

Use Liquid Applique to give the look of hand-cast paper: handmade paper molded into a pattern.

Using white Liquid Applique:

1. Stamp a large, simple design onto watercolor paper using a light pigment ink pad, such as light blue.

2. Apply Liquid Applique to the design. Do not cover up inner lines of the image as you will lose the design, but cover all outer lines and edges.

3. To add texture to the design, let the design dry for 2-3 hours. Then add details.

4. Let design dry completely overnight. This is *very* important.

5. Puff up the design with your heat source. If using a heat gun, do not heat too closely nor too long, to avoid scorching. Keep the heat source moving over the surface until completely puffed.

6. To add color, follow the directions above, using pigment ink refills.

▲ ▲ ▲

Glittery, glitzy paper
(see *Papers*)

Sealing Wax
Add sealing wax and seals to your stamping. Try it in collages, using stamped designs and unusual papers.

You can also rubber stamp into hot sealing wax, rather than using traditional seals.
▲ Use baby oil to oil the rubber and the underside of the wood mount of your stamp first.
▲ Then impress your stamp design into a mound of the hot wax you have just dripped on the paper.
▲ For an added effect, re-stamp the design on top of your first impression with gold pigment ink.

For special touches, glue items onto your designs to enhance the stamping.
▲ Add wiggly eyes to animals, eyes, cartoon characters, etc.
▲ Use them to animate an inanimate, stamped design.
▲ Get inexpensive Victorian findings, such as gold filigree items, to glue onto a Victorian card or sentimental Valentine.
▲ Use fine "angel shred" coming out of a stamped gift box or bag.
▲ Easter grass can be glued onto a card for "grass."
▲ Glue on dried flower petals, perhaps around a vase of stamped flowers.
▲ Put little bows on cards.
▲ Add jewels to your stamped creations:
  • Use the press-on "jewels" that come on a sheet, in many shapes and sizes.
  • Try a Be-Jeweler, by Creative Crystal Company.
    • A heat tool designed to pick up Creative Crystal's round rhinestones, heat it to the exact temperature for the adhesive backing to melt.

Adding
Extras

- Then place it where you want it.
- Works on both paper and fabric.
- Comes with different size tips to accomodate their different size rhinestones.

▲ ▲ ▲

Changeable Color Pens

There are different brands of these changeable markers, one of which is *Eye Popper Pens*.

A changeable pen is a marker with two tips: one end a broad chisel tip which is the base color; the other a round tip with the "pop" color which is applied over the base color. Within a few seconds, like magic, the color "pops" out.

The Eye Popper pens have 5 base colors and 6 pop-out colors. The white is the eraser. Color the background with a base color and use a special overwriter to change the color. In one case the overwriter appears to bleach out the background, and in another case, it changes blue to yellow, or dark blue to light blue, etc. All Eye Popper Pens work with any of the base colors. Brush the *"popper" color* directly on the rubber of the stamp and stamp onto the background.

Ideas:
▲ Color a solid background, and stamp a phrase as the "pop" out design.
▲ Solid rubber stamp designs look great stamped as the "pop out" design.
▲ To get a negative-like image, much like Andy Warhol's repeated images, stamp different color backgrounds on the paper, then stamp a portrait-type stamp on each background.

Basic Principles

The *art* of rubber stamping is not in the drawing; it's in the creating. Rubber stamping is very simple, easy and fun. You do not need to be able to "draw a straight line." However, it helps to know the basic art elements of color, composition, and perspective. For many of us, these elements come easy. By studying art, doing other forms of art over the years, or because it often comes naturally, we are generally applying these basic principles without much thought. These elements come in to play whether we are creating a complicated scene or a simple card with just one stamped element. It is often just the placement of a single item, or a color combination, that makes all the difference in an interesting composition.

Without often being aware of it, most "art," be it a store bought greeting card, an ad in a magazine, or fine art, is judged subconsciously by three elements. Is it *technically* well done; is the *composition* pleasing; and is it *appealing*. By knowing about, and executing, the first two elements, it is the third one that makes a truly interesting card. Be creative. Try something different...be it an unusual color composition, something that doesn't quite fit (I love putting a cartoon figure in the middle of a scene, for example), or an unusual placement of one element.

Color

Color sets the tone and mood of the art. Knowing how to use color can help in determining the mood you want. The right combination of colors will add interest.

Begin to notice colors and details around you. Stare at clouds and sunsets. Notice the colors you "really" see, not just what you expect to see (green grass, blue water). The more creative you are, the more things you notice... and the more you notice, the more creative you will be.

The weather and your mood can affect your color choices, even when you are inside and stamping something unrelated to the weather. On gray, cold days, colors tend to be darker and grayer. On bright days, spring and summer, the colors we choose are brighter, and scenes are cheerier.

▲ ▲ ▲

Primary colors

The primary colors, red, blue, and yellow, are the three colors that create all the rest of the colors.

Secondary colors

Purple, green and orange are made by combining the primary colors. Purple is red and blue, green is blue and yellow, and orange combines yellow and red. To get varying shades of these colors, more or less of one of the colors in the combination will yield turquoise, heliotrope, etc.

Tints and Shades

Tints and shades of colors are made by using whites and blacks. To get pink, you would add white to red; crimson comes from adding black to red. With only red, blue, yellow, white and black, you can mix any color you want. This is more true of some media than others.

If you look at the color wheel you will gain some basic knowledge of using colors together.

▲ ▲ ▲

The Color Wheel

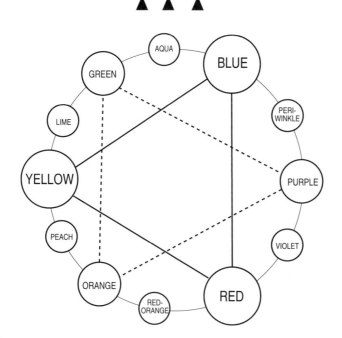

▲ Colors across from each other on the wheel are complementary colors. They make each other look most vibrant.
  - When these colors are placed side by side, they strike the eye with the greatest contrast.
  - Contrast is interesting when it is not used in excess.
  - In general, contrast should be in small areas, but within an overall harmonization of the whole.
  - There are times you may want to use this knowledge of complementary colors to clearly make a strong impact in your design.
▲ The colors next to each other on the wheel make each other look their best. The closer the colors are on the wheel, the better they blend together.

Colors can be labeled warm, cool or neutral.
- ▲ Oranges and yellows are warm colors.
- ▲ Blues, greens and purples are cool colors.
- ▲ Neutral colors are the beiges, grays.

Cool colors evoke the pale, winter sky, reflections in the water, the water or snow surface. Cool colors are serene, wintry, refreshing.

The warm colors imply a physical and emotional warmth. These are the golden colors of sunshine and sandy beaches. Warm colors are energetic, enthusiastic and welcoming.

All colors have their warm and cool sides to them. Most colors can be cooled by adding a touch of blue to them. So yellows with a touch of blue turn a cool limey green. Although blue-greens are cool, the rich greens with a strong touch of yellow are more warm than cool.

▲ ▲ ▲

Color Schemes

Different combinations of color:
- ▲ Complementary: colors directly across the color wheel from each other.
- ▲ Analagous: colors next to each other on the wheel.
- ▲ Triadic: colors that form a triangle on the wheel. For example, green, orange and purple are triadic.
- ▲ Monochromatic: using the same shade with different intensities (light to dark).
- ▲ Polychromatic: using many colors, used in realistic scenes, etc.

HOT

TIPS

Using Color in Designs
- *The color in a design usually becomes the focus of attention.*
- *The differences of tone, such as highlights and shadow, provide information about form, shape, texture.*

- *The proportions in which colors are used in a design affects the atmosphere of the piece.*
- *Light colors at the base of the design, with darker colors on top, give a top-heavy feeling.*
- *Strongly contrasting colors produce a more active impression.*

▲ Creating distance in stamped designs:
- Colors and images in the distance are more muted and less defined. Using the same inked stamp 3,4,5 times without re-inking will give this effect.
- Stamp one flower over and over for a field of flowers, a tree for a group of trees, etc.
- When re-inking the design, change intensity of colors, to give more feeling of depth.
- Stamp in the lightest color first, then re-ink in a slightly darker one each time, ending with the deepest colors in front. This will create the illusion of depth.
- Use different colors as well. If you are stamping grass, stamp in shades of green. Add a little teal blue, a little yellow or tan. Look at nature: you will see green grass isn't really all just one color of green.

▲ ▲ ▲

Light and Shade

To add depth and form, light and shade play an important part in a composition. The way light is reflected from a surface helps to identify the shape and form of objects. Light enables you to depict three dimensions on a two-dimensional surface. Being aware of where light is coming from and where it falls will change your stamping, especially in stamping out scenes and objects you wish to give a three dimensional appearance.

To determine the light and shade in a piece, you need to think about where the light is coming from. Follow the thought through as you color. The light will always reflect on the side the light is coming from. Highlights should be placed where the light falls on an object.

▲ ▲ ▲

Blending Colors

To add interest to solid-image stamps, use more than one color on the rubber before stamping. For example, a large sun will look good colored with yellows, oranges, a little hot pink. Start with the darker color markers. Apply to the edges, then work in with lighter and lighter markers. Use each succeeding light color to pull and blend the darker color just applied.

In working with nature stamps, such as a tree, put some dark green streaks on the image. Then color over with a lighter green, pulling the darker colors to the edge. Huff on the stamp before stamping and the colors will blend on the paper.

Blending colors like this also helps the look of the solid-rubber stamps when stamped on paper. Often the ink tends to puddle up on the stamp and create blotches on the paper. With blended colors, the blotching effect may not seem as notice-able.

Composition

To create a more effective composition, it helps to keep some basic art elements in mind.

Notice how sometimes a "chaotic image" can seem harmonious, and some simple stamping can seem chaotic. This key element is balance ... the sense of completeness you feel the art creates. If you have one predominant image on one side, then you can have several small ones on the other to balance. In the case of graphic design, a repetition of the same image can create a balanced effect.

▲ ▲ ▲

A picture, even a simple one, needs a focal point. The focal point is the main element of a design, where your eyes generally focus first. This determines if a work is "too busy," or if the elements complement each other. If your attention is pulled in different directions at once, it can be chaotic.

Once you establish from what vantage point you are creating the picture, you can then arrange your other images by size. Create interest, and set your composition off from an ordinary one by making your focal point something a little out of the ordinary, or slightly off-center.

▲ ▲ ▲

Perspective, an element in a good compositon, is the perception of an object in relation to its distance from the viewer. The closer you are to a subject, the larger it is. Therefore, a tree in the foreground will be huge as compared with mountains in the background.

Put bigger images up front, use smaller images behind to create distance. You may at times be looking for specific-sized

A Main Focal Point

Perspective

PERSPECTIVE

stamps for your focal point, or for smaller stamps for distance when you're adding to your stamp collection. Keeping perspective in mind, remember that your stamps are not, and should not be, all the same size. Stamps you felt "didn't go together" can often be combined. This will give you more versatility with your collection of stamps and gives interest to your compositions.

An aspect of perspective is "vanishing point." This is a "tunnel" effect: wide images narrowing to a point, like a road narrowing in the distance. The far distance image can be in the middle of the paper, or off to one side. Avoid having everything on the same horizon line,,, all in a row, all the same size. With perspective, you give the eye a place to go in the picture.

Scenery

Stamping out scenes is very creative and it incorporates all the principles discussed. It allows you to combine many of your images, often ones that you never thought could be used together. You can tell a story, even communicate a feeling. Use perspective to add depth, and color to add emotion.

Scene-making involves some planning, and employs the use of small details to add interest. I find this creativity addicting.

▲ ▲ ▲

Planning is the first step. You may already have a scene in mind. Or perhaps you just want to start a scene from a "blank canvas." Choose a favorite stamp, stamp it on your paper, then pick other stamps to include with it. You needn't have any preconceived ideas of what the scene is going to look like. Build the scene as you stamp.

Planning

To plot out a scene: On a large workpad, such as a pad of newsprint used as your work surface as well, experiment before finally putting the design on your paper. Using scrap paper such as the newsprint, stamp your scene as you wish it to be.

Visually break down the scene into three horizontal parts. Large images go in the forefront (masked when needed). The middle is the area to put things of added interest: trees, people, windows, furniture (inside and outside, both are considered scenes). The last is the background...mountains, skyline, clouds, wallpaper, etc. The horizon line should fall either above or below the middle of the composition.

One important element to scene stamping is creating the illusion of depth. This is easy with a little "trick." Keep in mind that the bottom of the paper appears to be the closest to the viewer. Therefore, images that are at the bottom will appear larger. Remember to anchor your largest images on the bottom, making the images smaller as you move up the page.

To give the feel of looking "into" a picture, put some large trees or vegetation at the bottom corners of the card. This will give the illusion of the viewer looking through a break in the trees to view the scene.

▲ If you're planning an intricate scene, stamp everything on your practice paper without masking. Just let everything overlap.
▲ It sometimes helps to use different colored inks to differentiate the images.
▲ From this, you will be able to see what needs to be masked at the final stamping on your cardstock.
▲ You can number your images from 1 to whatever, starting from the front. Start stamping and masking your actual project, following the numbers and the design on the pad. In doing a scene, remember "front first." In stamping a scene, you are working the opposite of painters. You will start with the front and work back. First, mask the image in front, and continue to work your way backwards, masking as necessary.
▲ When I say work from front to back, this is meant mainly for your large, main pieces. You can always go back to add in some touches to complete the scene, such as flowers, rocks, grass, sky.

▲ ▲ ▲

Color

Choose colors in your scene to reflect the season you're portraying. Winter is a lot of pale blues, greens, and lots of white. Light, pale colors depict spring. The grass has yellows and light greens. Flowers are bright and vivid. The sky is pale blues, greens, pinks.

Summer has darker greens, some browns showing in the sun-baked grass. The sky is bright, deeper blues with pinks. Fall is more intense browns, oranges, yellows, many shades of green.

Sky and Grass

You will see that there are no solid colors in nature. Depth is provided by the shades of the same colors you add, and the unexpected colors found in nature.

Trees

There are many fabulous trees in nature, and the different stamp companies have many trees to pick from. Don't limit yourself to one tree, or one type of tree. Vary the types in your composition, just as they are varied in nature.

Water

There are some wonderful water stamps on the market. They have various ripples and swirls. Stamp with your water stamp, then sponge over the stamp in lighter shades to get the feel of water. For an added touch, wet a small watercolor brush, and go over the area. This will soften the sponging.

Viewpoint

The viewpoint of your card is important. What do you want to stress? Should the card go horizontally to express a wide expanse, or vertically to show height? You do not need to see a whole design from ground to sky. Perhaps you are looking through the trunks of trees only. Or, looking over the tops of trees or buildings at the sky. (See *Scenery* in photo section)

Scene Stamps

I cannot write about scenery without talking about some great stamps that have revolutionized scene stamping for me. The stamps, from A Stamp In the Hand and from Stampscapes, are both by artist Kevin Nawasaki, and are designed to work together as interchangeable elements. They work in conjunction with other stamps as well. Their beauty is in the scenery they produce.

These stamps are meant to be colored on the rubber before stamping. Add several shades of colors to the elements in the scenes. For instance, trees can be shades of green, mountains may be purple and black, or brown and orange. The beauty of these stamps is their ability to take on different looks by the colors you choose. You can also experiment with stamping your entire scene in black, and coloring with colored pencil.

With these stamps, a lot of the work is done for you. Start with one large stamp as your focal point. Where you stamp it will influence what your picture is going to be. For instance, stamp a lakeside with trees high on the paper and you will have room for some "lake action," perhaps fishermen, boats, etc. Stamp the lakeside low on the paper to show a lot of sky.

Once your key element is stamped, decide what goes with it. Put in some large trees. I like to put my large trees on the side in front. This brings the scene forward, gives the illusion of depth, and breaks the horizon line. Add clouds, or a moon or a sun. What you add will determine the coloring and mood: a warm, sunny day, an eerie night scene, a cloudy afternoon.

Stamp mountains in the back, rocks or a waterfall in the foreground, frogs on a lilypad, or a fish jumping out of the water.

1

2

3

4

5

Dot Image Stamp

There is the magical "dot image stamp," another design by Kevin, referred to as "Field of Sky" by A Stamp in The Hand, and "Tonal Applicator" by Stampscapes. This stamp has the ability to tie all the elements of the scene together.

There are two ways of using this stamp for scenes:

▲ After the scene has been stamped, I go back over it with the dot stamp. Tap it up and down as you would a sponge (see chapter on *Backgrounds*). Use colors of the sky, such as blues, purples, pinks, yellows. Tap it around the card, working from the outside of the card in light to dark colors. This will blend all colors together in the scene and give a soft look.

▲ Or, especially for a sunset scene, tap the stamp as background before stamping the scenery. Bring in all the yellows, pinks, purples of sunset, working from lightest to darkest, from the outside in, in a circular pattern. The middle of the paper should be the lightest portion. The effect will be almost like looking into a hole. Then stamp your scene over this, remembering that at sunset all colors of the landscape are very dark.

▲ ▲ ▲

Using a brayer to make a scene background is one of my favorite techniques. The handcolored rainbow pads make beautiful sunsets.

Look for ones that have their lightest color at one end. For example, I like the Abracadada pad in "Carnival" for scenes. It starts with a yellow on the left side of the pad. Some of the others I use have their light colors at the right side of the pad.

1. Turn your pad so that the light color of the pad is on your left-hand side (if you are right handed).
2. Ink up with the light color on the left side of the brayer.
3. Begin rolling, placing the left side of the brayer running

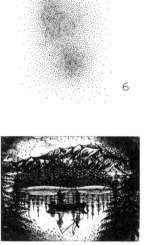

6

FINAL

Brayer

down the middle of the paper.

4. Roll the brayer up and down, and repeat until half the paper has a nice smooth look.

5. Re-ink the brayer, again with the light color on the left side of the brayer.

6. Turn your paper completely around, so that the blank half is to your right.

7. Placing the brayer with its left side up to and abutting the half you just inked, roll out on your paper, over and over.

8. You will now have your paper covered with rainbow colors. The lightest colors will be down the middle of the paper, with the darker colors going to the edges.

9. Using the paper either horizontally or vertically, you have the background for a sunset/sun-up. Stamp the scene.

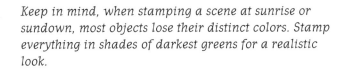

H O T

T I P

Keep in mind, when stamping a scene at sunrise or sundown, most objects lose their distinct colors. Stamp everything in shades of darkest greens for a realistic look.

H O T

T I P S

Tricks and techniques:

- *Off-center your point of interest.*
- *Use less colors at sunset or sunrise, when you really can't discriminate colors. I stamp mostly in dark green silhouette, as the eye does not discern color at this time of day. To give depth, vary the darkness of the greens...start with very dark and work to very, very dark.*
- *Winding roads give depth to a scene.*
- *Use cloud stamps with a powder blue stamp pad. Hero Arts has powder blue and PSX has wedgewood blue, both great light blue pads.*
- *There are stamps that "make" sky. Judikins, A Stamp In the Hand, and Alexstamping all have "sky"*

stamps.

- *Sponge in a sky. Marvy Marker color #60 is a good, light blue for this. Tap off the excess ink, so the blue is very light. (See chapter on* Backgrounds.*)*
- *Create the feel of sky through the use of images, such as birds, airplanes, buildings, planets, stars.*
  In stamping a scene, or any design, in which you may need an image you don't have, look at the parts of your stamps. In getting the most from the stamps you already own, you do not need to use the whole image. This also applies when buying new stamps.
- *Look at the parts of a stamp as well as the whole. You will see that some stamps may contain not only the design you want, but have design elements that can be used in part.*

▲ ▲ ▲

As mentioned in the discussion on trees, when you're in nature and looking around, you never see an entire scene at once. You cannot see the whole tree directly in front of you while looking at something in the distance as well. Your peripheral vision makes it impossible to see the complete image of things on the side.

Look at your finished card. Would a little cropping help it? The best way to test a scene is to make a right-angle mat of black paper. Move it around your card. Don't be afraid to cut off a little on the top or the sides of your finished product. Cut off part of the top if your sky seems to dominate the picture. Cutting off unnecessary space on the sides will bring the scene in closer to the viewer.

Cropping

OR

OR

You can use the techniques we just discussed in this chapter not just for scenery stamping. They apply to every card, every design you do. Not all the principles will always apply, but the same types of considerations are given to all artwork . . . even the simplest forms.

All of these, while being tried and true elements in art, are only guidelines. Being aware of the elements will help you compose your artwork. It will give you a basis to improve on something, if it "just doesn't look right." But they are only guidelines, not rules. Nothing is sacred . . . just create.

"Discovery consists of looking at
the same thing as everyone else
and thinking
something different."
—Albert Szent-Gyorgyi

Backgrounds

Every card, every decorated envelope, every postcard you stamp has a background. When you take one image and stamp it on paper, you may see only the stamped design. But "white space," the space left undecorated, is as important to your overall design as the stamped image. White space and balance are what make sense out of chaotic images, and what make one image "belong" on an otherwise blank sheet of paper.

Let's consider *white space*. To avoid the look of the design floating in space, consider the background space as part of your design. Often, off-centering the design, either placing the image slightly to one side or another, or a little higher or lower, will make all the difference in the world. Or stamp one or more images tilted in some unexpected way. Just a little unusual slant, or placement, can lift the card from ordinary to snazzy.

The trick to managing white space is *balance*. The total amount of white space and design space must balance each other. You can get a smaller image to balance a larger white space once you are aware of the entire space of the card, and judge the whole. You will be able to move an image around (in your mind, or by using the stamp without stamping) to find the right balance.

There will, however, be those cards that just seem to "need" something else. You can use background to add balance and interest. "Background" stamps should be included in *every* stamp collection. These can range from a stamp with random

specks, hearts, or stars to a "texture stamp" that is designed to produce a textured look. Textures can be fade-away dots, a marble or stone finish, checks, etc. A single small design can give you a great background.

HOT TIPS

For texture stamps or texture cubes used for a stamped background, choose light colors. Powder blue, light pink, yellow, lime green work well. Or use the rainbow pads, such as Abracadada's hand-colored pads.

For an unusual look, stamp a pattern from a texture stamp onto a large, solid area rubber stamp. For example, use a large balloon or a large, solid heart. Ink the texture stamp in a darker color and stamp it on a lighter-colored stamp with lots of inking area. Huff on the stamp and stamp on your paper. You'll get a design with a texture, or dots or squiggles, etc. Very fun, and quite effective for an unusual look.

There are many techniques and ways to obtain unusual backgrounds, scenes and textures, which we will look at here.

Tools for Beautiful Backgrounds

Cosmetic and other sponges, airbrushes, paper towels are other ways to get texture. They each have their own personalities.

▲ ▲ ▲

The most commonly used sponge to make backgrounds is the cosmetic sponge that comes in wedges, found in most drug and discount stores. A higher quality, denser cosmetic sponge, such as ones sold by Merle Norman stores, will give a more consistent look. But the technique for all wedge sponges is the same.

Sponges

HOT TIP

Be sure you work on a paper-covered workspace. I prefer using a newsprint pad, as they are very inexpensive and provide great workspace. When you are done with your stamping, you can just tear off the top sheet and throw it away.

Following the diagram for the wedge-shaped sponges:
▲ Look at the wedge as a right-angle triangle.
▲ Use your Marvy Markers to apply color at the middle top of the longest side.
▲ Try to avoid getting the color at the edges.
▲ Holding the sponge with your thumb and third finger on either side of the side with the color, squeeze the sponge. By doing this, the sides will curl upwards. This will prevent getting edge marks as you sponge, which produce harsh lines to your sponging.
▲ You do not want a lot of ink on your sponge, but rather a very dry sponge.

ADD COLOR HERE

HOT TIP *Save your Marvy markers that are drying up. They are perfect for coloring the sponges.*

▲ You can also go over one color with another color, working in many colors.
▲ For best effect, start with light colors and build up.
▲ Begin by tapping off some of the color on scrap paper. Tilt the sponge to get off as much as possible on the edges of the sponge. This way you will get a light, edge-free color and you can control the shading.

PAT STRAIGHT UP AND DOWN

▲ Tapping from the newsprint pad onto your cardstock inwards, tap-tap-tap onto your paper. Work from the edge of your card in. Pat hard and alter the pressure as you tap.
▲ Guide the sponge with your "eye" as you sponge. Look at the spot you are going to sponge, and tap the sponge up and down.
▲ Continue working until the color on the sponge dries up. Re-ink. Go over your work as many times as you wish to get the desired color intensity.

The technique of sponging can also be used to get textures such as grass, sky, water. (*See Scene Stamping.*)

HOT TIP *When sponging grass, combine grass-image stamps with sponging. First sponge your shadings to lay down the base colors. Use different color greens, blues and yellows to give the grass texture. Then use a grass stamp for the more distinctive blades of grass. Stamp the grass stamp over and over without re-inking to get depth.*

The following will give you different and unusual textures:
▲ The synthetic sea sponge, used in cosmetics, like Hero Arts' Silky Sponge, gives a wonderful airbrush look. Its texture provides a soft, authentic airbrush look to paper.

- ▲ Try natural sea sponges, kitchen sponges, loofah sponges and torn up cello sponges.
- ▲ Kids' sponges that come in unusual shapes, such as animals and alphabets.
- ▲ A kitchen sponge that has a brick-like texture will give a brick pattern.
- ▲ Sponge in clouds. Tear or cut paper or paper towel in the shapes you desire. Hold the cut paper down on your sheet, and sponge right over it. Keep in mind that clouds aren't just white. Sponge some light blue, a little violet over the white.
- ▲ Pick out small little clumps from the sponge. Do this helter-skelter all over the surface. Now when you sponge with it, using your light blues, you will get a cloudy sky effect.
- ▲ Tap Buff Puffs® onto a stamp pad. The fibers pick up very little ink and when they are tapped onto paper, the puffs leave small, light specks. The constant tapping between the pad and the paper builds up the depth of color you want.
- ▲ Nerf Balls and other soft, spongy balls give a great airbrush effect. Dab it onto an ink pad, or rainbow pad. Then lightly tap the inked Nerf ball onto the card. (Using Marvys on the Nerf ball shreds the pens.)

▲ ▲ ▲

Use templates with sponging:
- ▲ Rip an uneven edge in a long piece of paper. Lightly sponge along the edge. Move your stencil and angle it differently each time. You'll get the effect of a cloudy sky.
- ▲ Cookie cutters make good templates. Trace around the cutter on heavy paper, and cut out. Save both the parts of the cut out...the mask and the reverse mortise mask. Sponge around the one, or sponge the inside of the other. These look good as background designs for your stamping, and great on envelopes to use as a frame for the address.

Other types of sponges

Templates

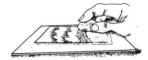

▲ ▲ ▲

Paper Towels

Paper towels can be used in different ways for different effects. It is another way to get an airbrush look, and can be used as a dabber to add color to backgrounds or to a stamped image.

▲ Bunch up a small section of a paper towel, making it about the size of a half dollar. Then squash it flat, color with markers. Tap it off just a bit, then begin to tap it up and down on your paper, like you would a sponge.

▲ Tear off a strip of toweling and wad it up so there is an area smaller than a dime to work with. Brush a marker onto the towel. Then spritz with water. Blot most of the color and water off onto a separate paper. Use the paper towel almost like a dry brush to swipe color onto mountains, sky, fill in water, a sun, etc. You can use more than one color at a time on the paper towel.

HOT TIP

Heavy-duty paper towels work great when doing faux finishes. The cheap paper towels shred easily and do not hold up as well. (See Faux Finishes.)

▲ ▲ ▲

Airbrush

Another way to get an airbrush look... with an airbrush. There are a couple of good airbrush tools on the market that are not as expensive nor as messy as the professional airbrushes.

▲ There are systems made by both DesignAire and LetraJet marker systems.

▲ Rather than mixing and messing with bottles of paint, color comes from markers. Each system will accept only its own brand of markers.

▲ An air hose is hooked up to a can of compressed air. You are blowing air off the markers with a can of propellant.

It may take a little practice to get proficient with this system. Always squirt onto a scrap paper first to make sure the air is coming through, and to get the pressure right. Aim the nozzle of the hose at the paper, not the tip of the pen.

You will find it a great technique for everything you do. Add color to images with this tool, as well as for backgrounds. This is a good way to make use of your templates...cloud templates, and any others you may want. Use objects such as leaves, a pastry basting brush fanned out, mesh, cheesecloth, etc. to get special effects with your airbrush. These will give unusual textures to your airbrushing.

▲ ▲ ▲

E. K. Success has a tool that will allow you to use almost any type of marker to get an airbrush effect, called the **Blitzer**. A rubber bulb is pumped to force air through the marker tip. The Blitzer will give you a very passable airbrush look and some different effects as well.

The Blitzer

▲ Use a narrow glue stick, such as one sold by Marvy and Hero Arts, instead of a marker. The Blitzer will spritz out glue in little splatters. Then pour glitter or embossing powder over your paper.

▲ There are accessory pens available for cake decorating, that come with blank nibs to add food coloring. Try adding glycerin instead. Then you can spritz the glycerin (like embossing ink) on your paper and emboss over.

Just keep in mind this is really more of a toy. Your hand will get quite a workout using it for very long. However, it is inexpensive (about $10), and a nice addition to add to your stamping tools.

▲ ▲ ▲

Brayers

A brayer is another tool that can be used for creating backgrounds. The brayer is like a paint roller, but the barrel is made of hard or soft rubber, lucite, or foam. It is attached to a handle, rolls like a paint roller and comes in different widths.

The soft rubber brayers, 3", 3 1/2", 4", are the best ones to use with the inks in stamp pads. They are very easy to clean. Just run them under running water. Clean them off with a soft cloth.

HOT TIPS

To store your brayer, keep it flat roller-side up, or upright. If the roller sits for a long time pressed down on a hard surface, it may develop a flat side.

Use a brayer to ink up oversized stamps that do not fit on your stamp pad. Just ink up the brayer, then roll over the stamp. Repeat this process as many times as is necessary to get the entire stamp inked up.

Be sure to ink the brayer all the way around.
▲ Roll it over the stamp pad in one direction.
▲ Lift, place it back at the top of the pad, and roll again in the same direction.
▲ By going in one direction, lifting and re-inking, you will ink the entire roller.
▲ NOTE: If, instead, you roll the brayer back and forth on the pad, you will only be inking about a fourth of the roller.

HOT TIP

There is no need to do this very, very slowly. I roll, lift, roll, lift many times, and I do it fast. In fact, I often see ink fly as I'm doing it!

After the brayer is inked, roll it on your paper.
▲ It can be used with all types of paper.

▲ Matte finishes allow the ink to roll on more evenly with no lines showing.

▲ Different papers will have their own personality, as you will learn.

▲ Be sure to have a large scrap paper under your work, as you will be rolling on and off your paper.

▲ Roll the brayer across the paper many times back and forth, re-inking if necessary.
   • It helps even out the ink distribution.
   • Again, there is no need to go very slowly.

HOT TIP

If you want to get rid of the harsh lines you get at the edges when you roll the brayer on your paper, first hold the brayer at a 45 degree angle to a piece of scrap paper. (This is where a newsprint pad under your work comes in handy.) With the brayer at this angle, you can roll the edges to take off a little ink from the very edges of the brayer. This will give a softer, fuzzier edge.

▲ On glossy paper, roll the brayer several times from different angles on the card.

▲ Use lighter colors for backgrounds.

▲ If you want pink paper to stamp on, and all you have is white, brayer up the paper with a light pink.

▲ If your background is brayered in a light color, you can color in the images you stamp. Use Marvy markers on all types of papers, or colored pencils on non-glossy paper. They are opaque enough to look good on a colored background.

▲ Get beautiful, effective backgrounds using rainbow pads, such as the Abracadada pads.

▲ To get continuous colored backgrounds with these pads:
   • Roll the brayer on your paper down the middle. You can roll straight or at an angle.
   • Turn the paper 180 degrees.

▲ Re-ink the brayer, and roll again, matching the colors end to end.

▲ ▲ ▲

Unusual brayered background techniques

Plaid

Use the beautiful rainbow pads to make a plaid background. First ink up the brayer and roll out in horizontal lines. Then re-ink, and roll in vertical lines. Use these for borders or backgrounds in layered cards.

With Stamps

Get a beautiful background of stamped images. Ink up a stamp and either:

▲ Roll the brayer over the stamp. Then re-ink, and roll the brayer over the newly re-inked stamp on another section of the brayer. Continue until the brayer has a pattern of stamps around the roller. Then roll the brayer over your paper. For a pretty effect, then over-stamp the image directly on your card a few times.

▲ Or, ink up the stamp and roll it carefully on the brayer itself. This works best with smaller stamps.

Paper Mask

▲ Lay a mask on your cardstock.
▲ Brayer over the card, remove the mask.
▲ You now have a blank image to stamp within.
▲ For example, mask out the inside rectangle of a card, which will give your card a frame.
▲ Stencil a large leaf for a fall motif. You can use this on envelopes, with the address inside the blank space.

Torn Mask

▲ Tear large pieces of paper in random designs.
▲ Tape each end on a scrap paper.
▲ Slip your cardstock under the taped papers.

▲ Roll your inked brayer over the card.
▲ When you have it colored as you like, pull the card out.
▲ The brayer will have left blank spaces where the masks had been.
▲ Now stamp your designs in the blank spaces.

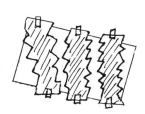

H O T

T I P

This same technique of using torn strips of paper as masks can be used with sponging, brayering (without the cheesecloth) and with textured foam blocks as well.

Color Wash
Use a brayer to put a wash of color over an area of a stamped card.
▲ Stamp your card.
▲ Tear a piece of paper (such as newsprint) raggedly.
▲ Secure the paper over a part of the paper, from end to end, as a mask.
▲ Ink your brayer with a soft color, and roll over the exposed section.
▲ When you take off the mask, you have a card with a light wash of color that is informally "swiped" across the center of the card. (See photo section)

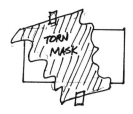

With Stencils
Use brayers over stencils with fairly large, open designs. Tape the stencil down and tape with removable tape. Then run the brayer over it.
▲ Great for making wrapping paper.
▲ Use with a checkerboard stencil and stamp in the small blank squares.

With a Mortise Mask
▲ Stamp out a name or design, using large outline alphabets or large simple designs. If you want the design even larger,

use a copy machine to enlarge.
▲ Cut out the design.
▲ Use the background paper as your "mortise mask," and the design you cut out as the regular mask.
▲ Place the mortise mask on the paper, and roll out a pattern from a roller wheel stamp, or colors with a brayer, or stamp into the interior space of the alphabet.
▲ Remove the mortise mask, and place the regular mask over the design you just brayered or stamped. With the mask in place, roll a dark color over the rest of the card or envelope. Use the mortise mask to add pattern to the inside of the letters or design.

Use of textures

For an unusual texture, use cheesecloth with a brayer.

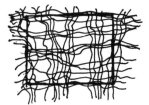

▲ Take a square of cheese cloth and remove a lot of the threads here and there to give you a more open pattern.
▲ Remove enough threads in each section to allow the brayered color to get through to the paper.
▲ Ink up a brayer on a rainbow pad.
▲ Lay the cheesecloth over the cardstock and apply the color with the brayer. The more you go over it, the darker the colors will be. Go in different directions to achieve new colors.
▲ When happy with the design, remove the cheesecloth.
▲ You can pick up the cheesecloth, re-stretch it, pick out more threads, and place it back on your paper as often as you wish.
▲ Works with other open textures, too. Look around. Try netting and other open-weave fabrics.

Resist

The brayer can be used to do a RESIST, which gives the effect of stamping light on dark. It often looks as though you stamped with bleach over a colored background.

With **embossing ink**

▲ Coat a stamp with embossing ink...either rolled on from the bottle, or stamped from a clear embossing ink pad.

▲ Stamp out your design on MatteKote paper. (This does not work as well on glossy paper.)

▲ Ink your brayer using a plain color or a rainbow pad.

▲ While the embossing ink is still wet, roll the brayer over and over on your entire paper, including the designs you just stamped. Do this until the entire paper is covered.

▲ Like magic, within a few seconds, the images stamped in clear embossing ink will "pop" out.

▲ The designs will not "take" the brayered ink, and it pops up almost white.

▲ This makes great "wallpaper" backgrounds. Use for layered cards. On light backgrounds, you can stamp, or stamp and emboss directly over this.

With **white embossing powder on white paper**

▲ Then brayer over this with rainbow ink.

▲ This works especially well with solid rubber stamps.

With **rubber cement**

▲ Rubber cement can be applied to your paper to act as a resist.

● Apply it with a brush to achieve a design, or

● Use a texture to apply the rubber cement with, such as crumpled up aluminum foil, or

● Use your palm, fingers, or bottom of your fist to apply the rubber cement to paper to achieve unusual textures.

▲ After the rubber cement has been applied, brayer over it with rainbow-colored inks.

▲ Let dry.

▲ Remove the rubber cement.

With **masking fluid**

▲ Put masking fluid in a fillable pen.

▲ Write your message.
▲ Brayer over the masking fluid.

▲ ▲ ▲

Unusual Techniques

▲ Put parallel strips of removable tape around the brayer.
▲ Ink the brayer. Pull off the tape. Then roll on your paper to get stripes.
▲ Use crepe tape, which comes in a variety of widths (made by Formaline or Chartpack) taped to your cardstock. The tape can be used to create all kinds of wavy lines, because it bends like crepe paper. Brayer right over your crepe-tape design. Let dry. Then lift off the tape and you have wonderful designs where there is no brayered color.
▲ Using colored markers, make slashes, dots, lines, squiqqles, etc. Then roll it out.
▲ For a Halloween or fall card, use the brayer with a rainbow pad, such as Abracadada's Harvest, or Alice in Rubberland's Painted Desert. Then stamp black, images such as devil heads, skeletons, spider webs, bats, etc. The background gives you a nice wash of fall colors.
▲ For a water-color look:
  • Use a foam roller (that you can get in a hardware store).
  • Ink up the roller with stripes, squiggles, dots, etc. Roll on your card.
  • Without re-inking, spritz the roller, and re-roll on the card. You will get a watercolor bleed.
  • This makes a beautiful, soft background.

▲ Carve a brayer to make your own roller stamp. Can use on paper, fabric and walls.

▲ For unusual TEXTURES:
  • Wrap Saran Wrap around a brayer to get interesting textures.
  • Brayer over dimensional textures, like bubble wrap.

- Put the bubble wrap on a flat surface, place your paper over it, and brayer the paper.
- Ink a brayer with rainbow colors and ink up a small piece of bubble wrap. Quickly invert the bubble wrap on cardstock and press down on it.

Brayering can be fun and creative. To help jumpstart your creativity, sit down with your brayer and pads and markers and brayer up a lot of cards. Try different techniques, different colors, patterns, etc. Put each card aside as you finish, and another day you can go back and use these cards as backgrounds for new creations. Consider this a play day. You will not be pressured to come up with the perfect background for a particular card.

Faux Finishes

Create the look of marble, granite, etc. to get unusual backgrounds and finishes for all sorts of projects. This technique is a lot like the finishing done on walls and furniture. The following are a few of the finishes you can achieve. Experiment with new ideas. Look around your environment at grains on wood, fabrics, colored marbles, etc.

Start with a base and add the finishing on top. This is done with a squished heavy-duty paper towel, Handi-Wipe, tissue (like Kleenex), or a sea sponge. Use glossy paper only, as it needs the smooth surface to swirl the color over the paper.

The Basics

The Base
▲ Crumple up a small section of the towel, tissue or sponge.
▲ Add marker colors—one or two colors—to the towel.
▲ Mist towel with water to dampen, then swirl. The more you swirl, the deeper the color gets.
▲ Re-apply until you get the desired depth of color.

Second Layer
Over the swirled background, lay down a texture.
▲ Using a towel or tissue:
  • Color a scrunched towel with markers.
  • You can leave the towel dry, or mist it .
  • Pat onto the surface, using an up-and-down motion like sponging.
  • The crumpled towel or tissue will give a textured look.
  • When your pattern becomes too repetitive, just re-scrunch the tissue and continue.

▲ Using a sponge:
  • You can get a texture by coloring a sponge with a very dry marker.
  • Tap off most of the color on a scratch paper.
  • Then pat over the base.

▲ Using a texture stamp:
  • There are many stamp companies that make wonderful "texture" stamps. Judi-Kins, for example, makes a stamp that imitates the scrunched paper towel look. It is aptly named "scrunch." There are many other textures as well that will give your piece different looks.
  • Color the stamp, stamp off some of the color, and stamp over the base.

▲ "Rag Rolling"
  • Scrunch up an entire tissue (this works best with a tissue) and roll it lengthwise.
  • Color the tissue, and roll it down the cardstock over the base color.

HOT TIP

Experiment with color combinations to get some beautiful backgrounds. If you have a stamped design you will be layering on this piece, pick colors to match or complement. The background will bring out the colors of the design.

▲ ▲ ▲

COLOR-ON-COLOR:
▲ Swirl color onto glossy paper for the base.
▲ With dry or wet towel, tissue, or sponge tap the same color
▲ over the first, letting the irregular pattern of the patting show over the more solid swirled background.
  For more pizzazz, use more than one color for the base coat or the colors scrunched as the top coats.

Using Craft-T Product's Gloss

1. Apply with your finger or sponge. I prefer using my finger.

2. Rub your finger (or sponge) into the gloss pot, then onto the swirled-markered base on glossy paper. (If you don't lay down a base of swirled marker first, the gloss colors will blend together and make "mud.")

3. Swirl on the gloss. Using your finger (or a sponge), buff the color as you apply it to get the look of metal. As you need more color, just dip back into the gloss pot and continue.

4. Add color on color to obtain highlights.

The Finishes

MARBLE

MARBLE

▲ Lay down a base coat of dark gray on glossy paper.
▲ Pat the same color over the first, as in color-on-color.
▲ Tear a small ragged piece of sturdy cardstock and color black marker on its torn edge.
▲ Carefully drag the colored edge over the gray tones to create "veining."
▲ For a gold veining in the marble instead:
  • Use a pigment style gold pen to make a puddle of the gold ink on a scratch piece of glossy paper.
  • Take the torn edge of a piece of paper and drag it through the puddle; then drag on your card for veins.

LAPIS

LAPIS

▲ Lay down a dark blue background on glossy paper. Pat with same color on top.
▲ For white veins, puddle up a white pigment pen, drag a torn sheet of paper through the puddle, and drag onto the blue base.

PATINA

PATINA

▲ Lay down a base with an olive green marker (such as Marvy #15).
▲ Use a dry or wet towel or tissue of the same color to swirl over the base.
▲ Using gloss from Craft-T Products Metallic Rub Ons®, swirl copper onto the markered background.
▲ Do not cover the entire piece with the metallic colors. Let the underneath colors show through.
▲ Go over lightly with gold metallic gloss.
▲ When completely through with the card (including any stamping and embossing you might do), spray with a matte fixative to seal.

VERTIGRIS

▲ Lay down a base with an olive marker (such as Marvy #15).
▲ Use a dry or wet towel to pat the same color over the base.
▲ Lightly pat some black on the base as well.
▲ Then swirl a metallic gold gloss over the card.
▲ When finished, spray with a fixative.

PEWTER

▲ Swirl glossy paper to make a gray base and pat the same color over it.
▲ Pat with either a wet or dry towel, tissue or sponge of the same gray.
▲ Rub it liberally with silver metallic gloss. Rub to a glossy finish.
▲ Add pewter and gunmetal gloss.
▲ Spray to seal.

BERYL-WOOD

▲ Use brown marker wet swirled on glossy paper for the base and top coat.
▲ Rub gold metallic gloss on the brown background.

GRANITE

▲ Lay down a dark gray base on glossy paper.
▲ Pat black marker over the paper with a crumpled, dry tissue.
▲ Re-apply, until the black is dense and dominant.
▲ Lightly sprinkle white embossing powder over paper and heat until dots melt on the surface. Use your fingers to sprinkle the powder, like adding a "pinch" in cooking.
▲ For other effects, try different colored embossing powders, such as a translucent gold, instead of the white powder.

VERTIGRIS

PEWTER

BERYL-WOOD

GRANITE

HOT

TIP

Be sure to heat from UNDER the paper so the powder does not blow off before melting.

MOTTLED EFFECT

MOTTLED EFFECT

▲ Lay a base of two or more shades of markers onto glossy paper.

▲ Spritz with Windex or water onto the paper, so that it spatters lightly and evenly.

▲ Or, spray into the air, and run the colored paper through the spray.

▲ Turn your card over. Using a pad under your work, blot off excess moisture carefully, without rubbing.

▲ Color will be lighter and spotty in spattered areas.

RESIST

RESIST

▲ Wet-swirl two or more colors on glossy paper.

▲ With a small paintbrush, paint on rubber cement or art masking fluid, making a pattern.

▲ Let dry.

▲ Swirl on more color until the pattern emerges clearly.

▲ Spray on water or Windex in a random, spatter pattern, for extra design.

▲ Blot off excess moisture.

▲ Rub off the mask.

WOODGRAIN

WOODGRAIN

Several stamp companies make a stamp that will give a "woodgrain" texture. The rubber is mounted on a rocker type of base. You can also find a version of this in paint and craft stores.

▲ Lay down your base color.

▲ For a wood look, use shades of browns, tans, light greens.

▲ To use the rocker stamp, you will need some practice.

- Roll the stamp over the ink pad.
- Start at the top of the paper, with the rocker positioned on the bottom part of the rubber.
- Apply pressure while rocking and dragging the stamp forward down the paper.
- Practice will help develop a smoothness to how you apply both downward pressure and forward drag.
- The results are well worth the practice it may take to get this technique to work as it should.

▲ Once you can work the stamp smoothly, try some variation on the amount of rotation, and perhaps a wiggle or two. You can get different looks that will give you the eccentricity of natural wood.

MALACHITE:
▲   Put down a base of dark green wet-swirled on paper.
▲   Then use black on the wood-grain stamp.

SILK MOIRE:
▲ Lay down a base color or two.
▲ Use a gold pigment ink pad on the curved wood-grain stamp.
▲ You will get a very credible imitation of moire fabric or ribbon.

▲ ▲ ▲

For Paper Antiquing:
▲ Use light colored recycled cardstock such as the parchment tans and grays.
▲ Rub Craft-T Products Metallic Gloss® over the paper with your fingers.
▲ Try copper, gold, light gold, pewter, silver on the paper.
▲ Rub on the paper, concentrating the deeper color at the edges. Because the paper is not glossy, the color will not glide across the card; you will need to work with it.
▲ The paper will get an old, yellowed antique look.
▲ Great for Victorian cards.

MALACHITE

SILK MOIRE

Paper Antiquing

Borders

Use borders around a design to add interest, and use up "white space."

▲ Small stamps can be repetitively stamped all around a card.

▲ There are many stamps made specifically for borders: checkerboards, small diamonds, checks, etc.

▲ Use a Post-it note to cover the middle of the card. Mask off the inside and then stamp, or use one of the finishes mentioned in this chapter to make a border.

▲ Do not consider a border as having to go around the outside of the card. Stamp your border in the middle of the card. You can make it slightly askew, or slightly to the top of the card. Then stamp within your border.

▲ With a border more in the middle of your paper, you can also stamp around the outside of the border, too. Example: Inside the border have a colorful scene. Outside, extend the scene in other colors, or in black and white.

▲ Stamps such as postoids, windows, etc. can be used as borders. Stamp within them, using many on a page.

HOT TIP

A border does not have to confine your stamping. Add interest to your design by letting some of the inside design "spill out" of the border. This will add interest and movement to your card.

Have some fun with the border by letting part of the design "peek out" from behind the border, or by going from the border into the picture.

Use your stamps to make backgrounds and borders with pattern stamping.

▲ Stamps are great for making repeating patterns.
▲ One stamp can be repeated over and over for a rich pattern.
▲ Don't limit yourself to "pattern" stamps. Any stamp might make a wonderful all-over pattern.
▲ In making patterned backgrounds, you do not need perfect, crisp images. You may want to obscure the images, make them fuzzy or unrecognizable. Your pattern of stamping may make your image not look anything like what it was designed as.
▲ Start with the lightest color in stamping multiple colors.
▲ Make your composition richer by adding darker colors after you have the light background.
▲ Use darker colors to make a border over the background.
▲ You can arrange your images:
  • horizontally, vertically, diagonally
  • curves
  • spirals
  • stamp at all different angles
▲ Combine pattern stamping with masking to put the pattern in the background as a border.

▲ ▲ ▲

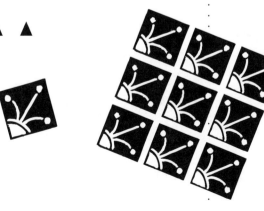

Making Your Own Paper and Patterned Paper

Using rubber stamps and playing with backgrounds leads to an interest in making patterned papers to use with stamping. There are many simple, fun techniques to add to the beauty of the stamping projects you do.

Of interest to many stampers is making your own paper. I will not go into the process of making paper in this book. There are many good books on the market, as well as some simple paper making kits you can buy.

There are ways, however, of using inexpensive paper you have at home to simulate some of the beautiful, expensive papers you see in fine art and paper stores. The following are easy ways to get pretty patterned papers, including marbeling, bubble paper, and paste papers.

▲ ▲ ▲

Crumpled Tissue Paper Paper

A fun and unique way of geting unusual paper involves common papers you probably already have around the house. You will need common bond typing paper (or Xerox paper, etc.) and tissue paper. Colored or patterned tissue make the best papers.

▲ Lay a piece of bond paper on a flat surface.
▲ On top of the bond paper, place a piece of cheap plastic wrap (not the kind used for microwave cooking). Freezer wrap wil also work.
▲ Take your tissue paper and crumple it up. Then flatten it out and place over the plastic wrap. Alternately, you could fan fold the tissue very tightly, or fold in any interesting

designs, then flatten out.

▲ Place a brown paper bag over the tissue to protect it..

▲ Heat your iron to its hottest setting. Do not use steam.

▲ When the iron is ready, place the iron on the brown paper bag covering. Move the iron around all the areas until the plastic wrap has bonded the tissue to the bond paper.

▲ You now have a crumply, interesting sheet of paper. Makes great paper to use for envelopes, and layers of a stamped card.

▲ For added interest, sprinkle sparkle or gold embossing powder on the tissue before ironing.

▲ ▲ ▲

Use any type of water-soluble paints or dyes for this. Leftover Easter-egg dye works well, as does food coloring.

There are two different methods of making the bubble paper. I call it the "inside," and the "outside" way.

For making bubble paper INSIDE the house:

1. Mix a squirt of dish detergent with colored water in a large shallow pan. Have a different container for each color you use.
2. Color the water with a dye such as food coloring, ink, or paints.
3. Use a drinking straw in the water to lightly blow lots of bubbles.
4. Take your paper and pass it through the colored bubbles in the pan.
5. You can do one color, or many colors on the paper.
6. Try different weights and different textures of paper.
7. Set the papers aside to dry.

Bubble Paper

It is recommended that the following method be done OUTSIDE on a calm day. Pick a day when it's not too windy.

1. You can use store-bought bubble solution, or follow this recipe:

H O T	Mix:	1/2 C. dish detergent
RECIPE		1 1/2 C. water
		1 T. light corn syrup

2. Divide the bubble solution into four containers, and add about 20 drops of different colored food coloring to each one. Adjust the color intensity the way you wish, remembering it will dry lighter. If the colors are paler than you want, add more food coloring until you get the brightness you like.

3. Lay out your paper on a newspaper spread on a driveway or deck. You can do many sheets at one time.

4. Blow the bubbles using a bubble wand across the papers. You want them to land and pop on the paper.

5. If you don't have a wand, try twisting a pipe cleaner.

6. Do not stand directly over the top of the paper, because the solution will drip onto the paper and cause blots instead of bubbles.

7. Allow the paper to dry.

With either of these methods, you can make some unusual paper, stationery and gift wrap.

The following easy instructions are for hand-marbeling paper.

1. Cover a table with newspaper to keep working surface clean.

2. Keep a small pile of newspapers at the side of the tray for drying your prints after coloring.

3. Use a large shallow plastic tray that is about 3" deep. Cover the bottom with about 1/2" of water.

4. Use acrylic or oil-based paints.

5. Add a few drops of turpentine or vinegar to the paint to thin it. Stir well.

6. Drop 2 drops of color onto the surface of the water. Drop 2 drops of another. Continue with whatever colors you want.

7. Let the droplets of paint fan out and cover the surface of the water tray (this takes a couple of seconds).

8. Slowly and lightly stir the color ONCE ONLY with a stick, toothpick or pencil to make a design.

9. Lay one edge of the paper on the water surface and lower the rest of the sheet. Or bow the edges of the paper so the center touches first, then let the edges fall to the surface. Either method will prevent air bubbles on the paper. The oil color is riding the surface tension of the water, so try not to push the paper below the surface.

10. The paper will take a print of whatever design the swirling color makes on the water surface.

11. Lift the paper off immediately and place face downward

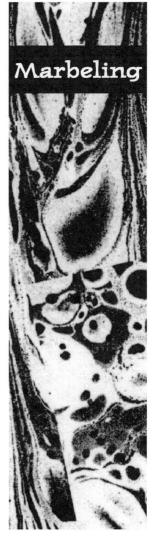

Marbeling

Paste Paper

onto the pile of newspapers at the side of the tray. This will absorb the surplus color and water from the paper.

12. It dries in seconds and can be stacked and weighted so that the surface will be smooth when dry. Or hang the papers to dry.

13. Repeat from #9 for further prints.

14. You can do this 3-5 times before you need to add fresh color droplets to refuel the swirling colors.

▲ ▲ ▲

You can get unusual textures, patterns and colors with an old-fashioned paste, brushed on paper. It's easy to make pleasing designs with little skill, yet you will have some very sophisticated graphic designs as a result.

To make paste paper, you will need:
▲ A shallow pan, or water nearby.
▲ A saucepan.
▲ 2 sponges.
▲ Small paintbrush, for mixing color into the paste.
▲ Large paintbrushes, to spread the mixture on the paper.
▲ A slick working surface: a sheet of plastic, formica, etc.
▲ Textures for making patterns in the paste: a plastic credit card, wood-graining comb, plastic forks, rubber stamps.
▲ Paper strong enough to be wet, such as water-color paper or 70-pound Canson or Strathmore drawing paper.
▲ Color from acrylic paints, poster paints, watercolors, gouache in a tube.
▲ Paste.

H O T

R e C I P e

The recipe:
4 T. flour	4 T. rice flour
3 C. water	1/2 t. glycerine
1 t. dish detergent	

1. Blend the wheat and rice flours together with a little of the water. Add the rest of the water and cook over medium heat, stirring constantly, until the mixture is like a thin custard. Remove from the heat and add in the glycerin and dish detergent to keep the paste smooth and workable.

2. Use a small brush to stir in 1-2 teaspoons of paint. Keep in mind that the paste will dry lighter than it looks in the bowl, so adjust the amount of paint to the color intensity you like.

3. Dampen the paper before applying the paste. This will keep the paste moist, and give you more time when working with making patterns. The best way to wet the paper is to place it in a tray, or the sink, with water. Let it get evenly wet and relax a few seconds. Take it out and let it drip a minute or two on a line of some sort.

4. Place the paper on your work area and stroke with a damp sponge to get out any air bubbles or excess moisture.

5. Dip your large paintbrush in the colored paste and brush on an even, thin layer of paste on the paper .

6. After the paste has been applied, drag your comb or pattern tool through the paste.

7. As the tool drags through the paste, it pushes the paste aside and the color of the paper beneath shows.

8. If your paste is too runny, the color will seep back into the pattern. If this happens, thicken the paste a little.

9. Make any type of all-over pattern you like. Have fun and be creative.
   ▲ Use large, solid-rubber stamps to make impressions in the paste.
   ▲ Use the "comb" to make random patterns, or more precise patterns, such as a basketweave.
   ▲ Use textured sponges to make patterns.
   ▲ Two sheets of paper can be covered with the paste.
   ▲ Press together and then peel apart. This will produce a feathery look to both pieces of paper.

10. You can also add bits of torn up magazine pages, gift wrap, cancelled stamps (they don't really have to be cancelled!), confetti, flower petals, etc. Add these after patterning. Seal with a thin layer of paste. Experiment with this, as it adds a lot to the finished paper.

11. Depending on the thickness of the paste, the paper will take time to dry. The paper may curl. If necessary, when it is completely dry, it can be ironed on the wrong side, or pressed flat under heavy books.

▲ ▲ ▲

Hand-Dyed Paper

The following are ways to dye ordinary paper, giving the look of expensive papers found in specialty stores.

There are different ways to get a blended tie-dye look.

Tie-Dye Effect

With Marvy Markers
▲ Unfold a napkin.
▲ Use markers to make slashes of colors all over the napkin.
▲ Leave some space between the marks, as the ink will bleed.

- ▲ Fold up the napkin.
- ▲ Spritz with water, getting it uniformly wet.
- ▲ Put the napkin between two sheets of wax paper and push the color through all the layers.
- ▲ Unfold the napkin carefully. If it is difficult, blow on the napkin gently as you unfold it, using your breath to gently force the napkin to unfold.
- ▲ While still wet, press the unfolded napkin on glossy paper to transfer the design on the napkin onto the cardstock.

Calligraphic Inks or Liquid Watercolors

- ▲ Fold 2 napkins together into a small shape.
- ▲ Spray the napkin to wet it, as in the steps above.
- ▲ Using droppers, drop different colored inks on the napkin.
- ▲ Unfold carefully after the color has bled on the entire napkin.
- ▲ Turn over and transfer the pattern onto glossy paper while still wet.

▲ ▲ ▲

For an easy background paper anyone can make, try this watercolor technique.

Water Color Effect

1. Soak a large sheet of heavy, white paper, such as bristol or watercolor paper, in water until it's saturated. This usually takes about 10 minutes. Remove the paper from the water and dab off any excess water with a kitchen towel.

2. To tear the large sheet into cards, it is easiest to divide the paper into strips, and the strips into card sizes. Fold the paper gently where you wish to cut and gently pull apart (The *wet cut.*) The result will be a most effective deckle edge to the cards.

3. While the cards are still damp, cover them with a diluted watercolor wash, paying particular attention to the torn

edges of the paper where the wash should be brushed in well.

▲ Use watercolor paint in little tubes.

▲ Put a little dab in a plastic dish and add water.

▲ The less color and the more water, the more diluted, antiquey look to the paper.

▲ Or use watercolor ink, such as FW, Acrylic Artist Ink, Pearlescent Liquid Acrylic, Waterproof Higgins Ink, or Rotring Artist's Color. These do not need to be diluted.

4. The length of time you leave the watercolor on the cards before you rinse them under cold water will depend on the darkness of the color you want, from 30 seconds to a minute or so. Most of the color from the center of the card will be washed away when you run it under the cold water, leaving the most color at the edges.

5. If you want a folded card, fold before it is perfectly dry, and place under a heavy object to finish drying. This makes the folding easier, and the fold will be perfectly flat.

▲ ▲ ▲

Hand-Dyed

Based on the Japanese art of "Orizomegami," it has been adapted for rubber stamping by Nancie Waterman of *Vamp Stamp News*. The original method involves precise folding and dying. For rubber stamp art, the paper can be dyed more randomly if you choose.

You will need:

▲ Ink: food colors, waterproof calligraphy ink, Liquitex acrylic paint.

▲ For glitz: metallic crayons, pearlescent calligraphy ink by Luma, or Liquitex acrylic iridescent tinting medium to mix with acrylic paint.

▲ Absorbent paper with wet strength, such as coffee filters, paper napkins, uncoated paper, or rice paper.

▲ Water
▲ Small cups, such as muffin tins, yogurt or pudding cups
▲ Plastic spoons
▲ Straws cut in 3" pieces
▲ Aluminum foil
▲ Newspaper and waxpaper to cover work area

1. Set up your work area:.
   ▲ Spread out newspaper and lay wax paper on top to cover your work table.
   ▲ Fill the small containers half full with water.
   ▲ Set out your ink, any glitter you want to use, your paper and straws.
   ▲ Add colored inks to the containers. Use 2 to 3 colors or more.

   For food coloring or calligraphy ink:
   ▲ Start with a couple drops of color in each cup. You can always add more if you want a darker color.
   ▲ Use either the dropper if it comes with the ink, or use a 3" straw as a dropper.

   For Liquitex acrylic paint:
   ▲ Squeeze out a small ribbon of paint into the cup.
   ▲ If you want to use the Irridescent Tinting medium, add half a spoon full now.
   ▲ Stir. (You'll need to stir occasionally, as the tinting medium tends to settle to the bottom.)

2. To dye the paper:
   ▲ Fold, crumble, or wad up your piece of paper. Make sure that part of it is small enough to dip into the small cups.
   ▲ Dip the small section into a container with the colored ink.

If the folded paper is dampened before dipping in color, the absorbency will be increased and the resulting color will be softer in appearance.

▲ Lift it out and squeeze excess dye back into the cup.
▲ Dip another portion of your paper into a new color.
▲ Fold and unfold to expose new areas of the paper.
▲ Keep dipping until the entire paper is dyed in the various colors. You can leave some parts uncolored.

Dip your paper randomly into the different colors. You needn't have any planned pattern.

3. Let the paper dry:
   ▲ After you have finished dying each piece of paper, unfold and lay it on the wax paper.
   ▲ Very thin papers, like napkins, may have to dry some before unfolding. Because these papers are so thin, they may tear a bit. Don't worry, in the mounting stage, you'll usually be able to "fix" it! (See *Mounting Lightweight Paper* later in this chapter.)
   ▲ You can let the papers dry right on the wax paper. The thinnest papers may dry in an hour, while the heavier papers will take overnight.

4. Add glitter, if you wish:
   To use Pearlescent calligraphy ink:
   ▲ Place the dried, dyed paper on the wax paper.
   ▲ Shake up the ink in the bottle.
   ▲ Use a straw to drag the ink over the paper; or blow through the straw to get glitter randomly over the

paper; or drip a few drops on the paper, then crumple it up.

▲ Add random color to the dyed paper by splattering acrylic paint with a toothbrush over it.

▲ You can stamp and emboss right on the hand-dyed paper.

▲ If your paper is exceptionally wrinkled or twisted, you may want to iron it between 2 sheets of wax paper.

5. Your paper is now ready to use. However, if the material you worked on is too lightweight to use on its own, you will need to bond it to a heavier base. (See section below on *Mounting Lightweight Paper.*)

HOT

TIPS

Tips, Tricks and Techniques:

- *Use surgical gloves while dying the paper, as the inks really stain your hands. Or use Lava soap.*
- *Use at least 2 or 3 different colors. Do not use colors that will not blend well. For example, red and purple will blend into "mud."*
- *When mixing colors, the water will turn the dyes lighter. Red will turn pink, dark blue will be a light blue. Some light colors, such as yellow, may not show up at all. It depends on the dye, and on the paper. If the color is too pale, add more paint.*
- *Experiment with patterns while coloring:*
  - *Take a round coffee filter and dip the center in a red dye. Then dye the edges blue. Where the two colors meet they will blend to a purple. When the paper is unfolded you will have a red center, blended to purple, and then to blue outer edges.*
  - *Take a round coffee filter and fold a few times, to get a pie-shape. Dip the center in one color. Then carefully dip the long folded edges in another color. When unfolded, there will be a starburst design.*

Mounting Lightweight Paper

Lightweight paper used in hand-dying may be too thin to use without mounting on cardstock or sticker paper.

▲ Use a piece of cardstock sprayed with spray adhesive or sticker paper large enough to hold the entire dyed paper.

▲ Carefully lay the patterned, lightweight paper over the adhesive-covered card or the sticky side of the sticker paper.

▲ Starting in the middle of the card, smooth the paper from the middle to the edges.

Smoothing or burnishing papers:

▲ Helps to sharpen a crease or fold and bond glued papers.

▲ It also helps to push out wrinkles and eliminate air bubbles trapped between glued papers and the boards they cover.

▲ To avoid damaging or shining the paper, cover it with a sheet of waxed or tracing paper.

▲ Hold the burnisher on its side and smooth from the center of the sheet outward to flatten.

▲ Or, use a hard brayer to make a really smooth contact with the dyed paper to the sticky surface. After smoothing down the paper with your hand, run a brayer over the entire surface.

▲ Papers that have been stretched by gluing will shrink as they dry and tend to warp the paper they cover. To prevent this, place your bonded paper between sheets of waxed paper and place between two heavy books.

▲ If your piece has torn while dying, combing, folding or otherwise working on it, now is the time to "fix" it. Carefully butt the edges next to each other as you bond the paper to a sturdier piece. You should not be able to see the tear after mounting.

▲ ▲ ▲

Weaving paper strips into patterns is a way to recycle and make beautiful backgrounds. You can use paper that you have stamped and were going to throw away, as well as using some of your pretty papers. Since the paper is going to be cut in strips and woven, you can use papers that aren't "perfect."

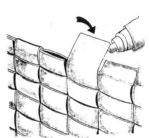

To weave:
▲ There are the warp strips (the ones that are put down first, side by side); and the weft strips, which are slotted in and out, over and under the warp strips.
▲ Cut a number of paper strips. They can be any manageable size and from 1/4"-1/2" or so wide. Cut the weft strips slightly longer than the warp, as these will be woven in and out.
▲ Leave the warp strips side by side on your work surface. Weave a weft strip through the warp strips. Start by passing it over the first warp strip, under the next, and so on. Start the second weft strip by passing it under the first warp strip. Continue weaving in this way. Gently push the weft strips together.
▲ If the warp strips slip, anchor them to the first weft line with paper clips or weigh them down with a heavy book.
▲ If a strip is too short, lenghten it by joining it to another strip. Overlap the ends of two strips and glue together.
▲ Make sure the join falls on the wrong side of the weave.
▲ When you have finished, secure the ends. Fold them crisply to the wrong side along the edges. Trim, leaving a turn the width of one strip. Spread adhesive, such as a glue stick, on the back of the turning and press to the wrong side.

For Interest:
▲ An even basketweave is the simplest. All the strips will be approximately the same width.
▲ To add interest, make the strips different widths.
▲ Vary the color and patterns of the strips.

▲ Vary the textures of the paper strips. But try not to vary the weights of the paper.

▲ Combine strips of magazine and newspaper pages.

HOT TIP

When using newspapersn in your paper weaving, spray with a fixative before handling to prevent smudging.

To Use:

▲ The woven sheets can be attached behind window frame cards.

▲ They make a good background, applied to a base card. Put stamped images over it with double-stick tape, or foam tape.

▲ ▲ ▲

Collages

Collages are another way to make good use of your mis-stamped projects, and various scraps of paper. You can also use the back of your mis-stamped papers to stamp, as these will be glued down!

Simply tear your papers up into unusual shapes. Use the *wet tear* method to get some ragged ends, as well as using any edging scissors, punches, etc.

If you are working with very thin materials, such as tissue paper, the glue you use will be important. You do not want the glue to seep through the papers. Yes glue and Letraset's Studio Tac (*see Adhesives*) both are excellent for this.

▲ ▲ ▲

With all of these beautiful papers, you will want to use them with your stamping. Some of these papers can be stamped on directly. Others will be layered with stamped designs, using different colors and patterns as a base for interest.

Layering sheets of paper is an effective way to use color and dress up a stamped card. This resembles the look of a matted picture. Lay your stamped card stock on a larger sheet, or sheets, of colored, patterned paper. Use the base card to pick up the colors in your stamped design. This will offset your design and make it look like a more complicated piece than it actually is!!

Before permanently afixing the papers, play around with sizes, colors, and shapes of the pieces, and the placement of the whole. Once you are happy with your composition, adhere each piece to the next.

Give layers a unique edge using the fancy scissors, You can get a scalloped, wavy, pinking, or serrated edge with the scissors. Or use the wet paper technique to get a deckled edge.(See the section in *Backgrounds* on cutting.)

Layering is good for "fixing" mistakes. If, after a lot of work, you get ink smudges on part of the paper, why not cut out the part of the paper that is smudged? Mount this new-sized paper on layers of colored papers. This "new," unplanned card, may come out better than the one you had originally planned!

Layering

Beyond
The Basics
Color Photos

**Terms in bold print refer to techniques
that appear throughout the book**

Papers

1. Angel (Paper Garden) embossed on **transparency film for laser printers**, and colored with **Zig Super Clean Color** markers to give the look of **Stained Glass**. Layered on white cardstock and framed with black glossy cardstock.(MA)

2. Lady (Dottie's Darlin's) stamped on **bristol paper** and **watercolored**. Happy Birthday (PrintWorks) embossed in black. Layered on pink glossy paper, then a sheet of white cardstock **brayered** with lagoon Abracadabra rainbow pad.(MA)

3. Snowman (Northwoods Stamps) embossed and colored on separate cardstock and cut out. Adhered, using the **paper tole technique**, over cardstock embossed with snowflakes (Northwoods Stamps) embossed in light blue.(Card by Pat Niemuth)

4. Fish (Hot Potatoes) stamped in black on white cardstock and embossed in pinks and purple tinselette embossing powder (Enchanted Creations) layered on green and pink **bristol paper** colored with **water-color dying technique**.(MA)

5. Stamps (Dottie's Darlin's) embossed in black, lady done with **watercolor**, on **bristol paper** colored with the watercolor dying technique.(MA)

6. Saying (Arizona Stamps, Too) embossed on pink **watercolor dyed bristol paper**. Edges deckled with the **torn paper technique**, and layered on black linen with same edges.(NJ)

7. Background card is white glossy cardstock **tie-dyed with markers**. Thanks embossed in black over background. Hibiscus (both stamps Judi-Kins) stamped, colored and adhered by **paper toling**.(MA)

8. White **mulberry** envelope stamped with ferns (Stampendous) using green markers.

9. Three panel card cut with frames. Inserted in the frames are sheets of **transparency paper for copier** with girl (Paper Garden) and table (Stampa Barbara) copied onto it, and colored with **stained glass paints**. Border of card **airbrushed** in multiple colors, and **texture stamp** (Stampendous) stamped in black. (Card by Suze Weinberg)

10. Thank you (TooMuchFun) embossed in black on pink **watercolor-dyed bristol paper** layered on pink **mulberry paper** with **wet-torn deckled edges**.(NJ)

11. Kraft colored cardstock **dry embossed** with leaves. Leaf (Hero Arts) embossed with copper on cardstock, layered on natural paper and black line both **wet-torn deckled**. (MA)

12. Beige **watercolor dyed bristol paper** embossed in copper with border design (Hot Potatoes).(NJ)

13. **Mulberry paper** folded according to instructions for **envelope #3**. A triangle of gold **Momi** paper attached for extra interest.

14. **Hand-dyed paper** used as book cover. Embossed in black with Just for You (PrintWorks) and rose border (Touche) directly on paper. (MA)

Papers:
a) **Hand-dyed**; b) **crumpled tissue paper paper**; c.) white **mulberry paper**; d) **bubble paper**; e.) **hand marbled paper**.

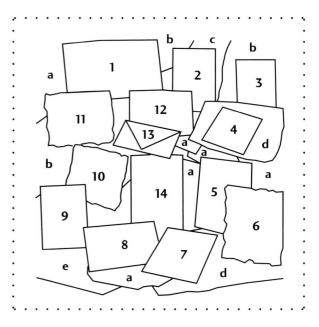

Cover: Scenery stamps by Stamp In The Hand. Card by Michele Abel.

Note: Unless otherwise noted, artwork in the following pictures by: **MA**, Michele Abel; **NJ**, Nancy Jordan; **CB**, Carla Barrett.

Album Page

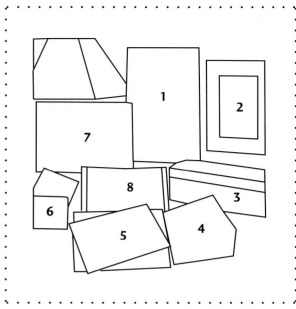

1. **Calendar** done with photos and stamped images (Rubber Baby Buggy Bumpers), then **color copied**. (MA)

2. Photo transferred to glossy white cardstock with **Photo Phinish technique**, colored with markers; small group of flowers stamped onto the card. Then matted and framed. (MA)

3. Wood box stamped with black pigment ink, colored with colored pencils. Entire box was then finished with 7 coats of boat varnish. (Lesle Margolis, by Impressions in Inc.)

4. **Album page** is black linen, embossed in gold with picture frames (Stampa Barbara), daisy and "Simply the best" (PrintWorks). (MA)

5. Frame and stars is white cardstock with metallic **faux finish** using **Craft-T products metallic gloss**. Picture inserted behind and layered on black glossy cardstock. (MA)

6. Kodachrome slide stamps (Judi-Kins) embossed in black on cardstock and cut out. Pictures inserted behind, and layered on black linen **album page**. (MA)

7. Photo transferred to white glossy cardstock with **Photo Phinish technique**. Paper masked and **brayered** with a **color wash** using ambrosia Abracadabra rainbow pad. Layered on black, then on black floral **crumpled tissue paper paper**. All this is layered on cardstock that has been **airbrushed** in various colors, through the **bristles of a pastry brush**. (MA)

8. Pocket **calendar** stamped with flowers (PrintWorks) for the month of April. (MA)

Glitter

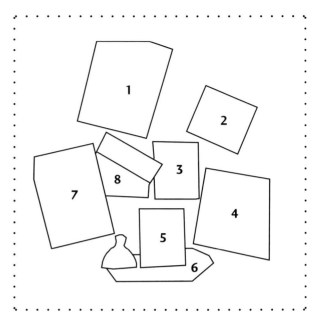

1. All images (Hot Potatoes) stamped with black pigment ink, embossed with various colors of tinselette by Enchanted Creations—except pots, which were stamped with Terracotta and Tapestry embossing powder by Ranger Industries. Images were cut-out and adhered to white glitter paper with varying layers of double-stick foam tape. Then this was all layered on green glitter paper, black glossy cardstock, and gold glossy cardstock. (MA)

2. Zebra (Judi-Kins) embossed with Terracotta embossing powder (Ranger Industries), Thanks (Judi-Kins) embossed with gold, and greenery embossed with various green tinselette (Enchanted Creations). All were cut out and affixed to black linen paper with double-stick tape. Layered on gold glitter paper, green glitter paper, black glossy cardstock, and gold glossy cardstock.(NJ)

3.Paper bags (TooMuchFun) stamped and embossed on paper bag and cut out. A small star punch was used to punch out stars on bags, then layered on green glitter paper to look like luminarias, with irridescent shred stuck behind bags and adhered to white, glossy cardstock with saying (TooMuchFun) embossed in black. Layered on strip of green glitter paper, kraft natural paper, red glitter paper, and black glossy cardstock.(MA)

4. All images copied onto **Drafting Applique Film** (see *Copiers*) and affixed to various colored glitter paper, then cut out and layered on white glossy cardstock, with a strip of black cardstock for flooring. Stamps (Posh) in background stamped with colored markers directly on cardstock. Layered on green glitter paper. Corners cut by **corner-rounder** (see *Cutting Techniques*.) (Card by Suze Weinberg)

5. All images (Posh) stamped with Enchanted Creations **Stamp-it Bold foil adhesive**, and foil applied to adhesive (see *Foil*). Cut out and layered on purple glitter paper, then silver glitter paper. Thanks hand-written using Enchanted Creations **Foil Writer** and foiled. (Card by Dee Gruenig)

6. Fabric napkin stamped with Hot Potatoes flowers and leaves using Deka **fabric paint**. (Hot Potatoes)

7. Vase, roses and leaves (Hot Potatoes) embossed on white glossy cardstock with various colors of tinselette embossing powders (Enchanted Creations), all cut out and arranged on blue glitter paper with double-stick tape. Layered on green and silver glitter paper. (MA)

8. White cardstock cut with wavy blade of **Fiskars paper cutter** and embossed with PrintWorks saying, layered on black linen paper. Apple (Rubber Stampede) embossed on red glitter paper and adhered with double-stick tape. Matching black linen envelope has apple (Hero Arts) embossed on red glitter paper, leaf on green glitter. The apple and the strip of green glitter paper are adhered using the glitter paper's self-adhesive back. (NJ)

Scenery

For complete information on techniques for these cards see *Scenery, Background and Basics*.

1. Background stamp (Rubber Baby Buggy Bumpers), moon (Arizona Stamps, Too), and zebras (Love You To Bits) embossed in black on white mattecoat (JudiKins) paper. Background colored in with **chalks** (Craft-T Products). Layered on silver glitter paper, then on white glossy paper with zebra print (Arizona Stamps, Too) embossed in black and layered on black glossy paper. (NJ)

2. This 3-layered card uses foam dots (Rubber Stampede) to attach each layer. The top layer is Christmas Houses (Rubber Baby Buggy Bumpers) stamped with dark blue pigment ink on white glossy cardstock. Second layer of trees (Arizona Stamps, Too) embossed in blue. Back layer is white glossy cardstock, **sponged** with dark blue, then mountains (A Stamp In The Hand) embossed with white embossing powder, layered on silver glitter paper. The first two layers have white **Liquid Applique** added for snow. (NJ)

3. All stamps by A Stamp In the Hand (designed by Kevin Nakagawa), colored with

markers directly to the rubber. Sun "swiped" in with yellow marker on a **paper towel**. Sky then blended with Field of Sky (A Stamp in The Hand), a **dot-patterned stamp**. (MA)

4. Center images (A Stamp in The Hand) stamped with markers. Additional color **airbrushed** in with Letrajet system. Border stamped with black African images (Kidstamps), and lines hand drawn. Layered on black and dark yellow glossy cardstock. (CB)

5. Background mountains (Rubber Baby Buggy Bumpers) embossed and colored with markers. Architectural stamps (A Stamp In The Hand) embossed in black and colored with Craft-T Products **metallic gloss**, then cut and layered on background with double-stick foam tape. Mrs. Bon Voyage (Rubber Baby Buggy Bumpers) embossed in black and colored with markers, then mounted on steps.

6. All stamps (including the zebras by Love You To Bits), and techniques done like card #1. (NJ)

7. All scene stamps by A Stamp in The Hand, following same technique as in #3. (ASITH)

8. Images (A Stamp in The Hand) stamped and embossed on white cardstock. Colored in with Craft-T Products **chalk**. Layered on black, pink, and black glossy cardstock. (MA)

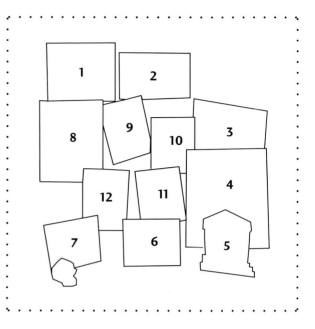

9. Trees (A Stamp in The Hand) stamped on bottom of white cardstock. Clouds and balloons **airbrushed** (with Letrajet System) using **templates**. Girl with balloon (Paper Garden) embossed on separate cardstock, cut and adhered with double-stick foam tape. (MA)

10. Garden scene (Stampendous) stamped and colored with markers directly on rubber of stamps. Then scene was cut in fourths (using a **Personal Trimmer**), slightly separated to give the illusion of a window and mounted on black cardstock, then bright yellow. (NJ)

11. White glossy cardstock **sponged** with medium blue.

Snowflakes (Hero Arts) embossed with white embossing powder. Snowman (Hero Arts) stamped, embossed and colored on separate cardstock; leaves stamped with green pigment ink and embossed with clear embossing powder. (MA)

12. Background **brayered** with carnival Abracadabra rainbow pad, **edges deckled**. Trees and grass (A Stamp in The Hand) embossed in black, sun (JudiKins) embossed with white embossing powder. Layered on black glossy cardstock, then on **brayered paper**, and then again on black glossy cardstock. (CB)

Backgrounds

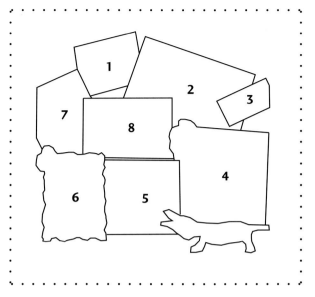

1. **Patina faux finish** background layered on a deckled white card and a black glossy card. Congrats and Checkerboard (PrintWorks) stamped in black pigment ink directly on faux finish and embossed with clear embossing powder. Statue and pedestal (A Stamp in The Hand) embossed in black on separate glossy paper, cut out and mounted with double-stick foam tape. (MA)

2. Wrapping paper with map design is mounted on deep red cardstock from Printworks. A **texture stamp** (JudiKins) was embossed on the cardstock. Sun stamp (A Stamp in The Hand) embossed on natural paper. Arrow (Stampacadabra) and globes (HA), stamped on separate paper and mounted, along with postal stamps from Herbarium. (CB)

3. Alligator (Graphistamp) stamped in black and colored with **colored pencils**. Layered on corrugated paper from Printworks. (CB)

4. Panda (Arizona Stamps, Too) stamped with black pigment ink and embossed on glossy paper. Leaves (Hot Potatoes) stamped with black pigment ink and embossed with various colors of green tinselette embossing powder from Enchanted Creations. Layered on corrugated paper from Printworks with raffia, and then layered on glossy paper, **brayered** using the technique of **dots, dashes, and lines** on the marker. (See section on *Brayers*.) (NJ)

5. Sunflowers and vine (Rubber Stampede) embossed on natural paper, and watercolored. Cut out and attached with **Paper Toling** technique, on natural paper cut with a deckle-edge scissors. Layered on black and deep yellow glossy paper. (NJ)

6. Victorian woman (Stamp Francisco) embossed in black and watercolored, on bark paper purchased from art store. Colored in with **watercolors.** Layered on handmade green paper. (NJ)

7. Mermaid (A La Art) stamped in black on Mattecoat paper (JudiKins) and **watercolored**. Paper was cut with a **deckle-edge scissors** and mounted on a strip of gold **Momi paper** (see *Papers*), layered on paper done with **faux finish** and gold glossy paper. (MA)

8. Thanks and Checkerboard (PrintWorks) embossed directly on **fun finish** card, mounted on a natural paper, black glossy paper and corrugated paper from Printworks. (MA)

Dance Party

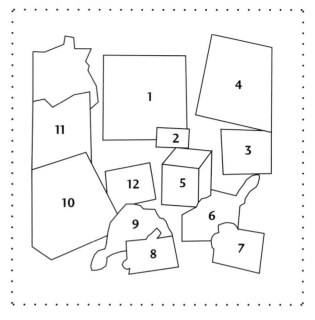

1. Invitation done with **Print Artist** on **computer** and colored with markers. Cartoon characters (Rubbberstampede) embossed and colored with markers on separate glossy paper, cut out and adhered with double-stick foam tape. Backed on red glossy paper and silver **glitter paper.** (MA)

2. Bugs Bunny embossed and colored on separate sheet of glossy paper. Cut out and affixed with double-stick foam tape to glossy folded gift card. Hand-drawn border and printed name. (NJ)

Fall Party:
All leaves by Hot Potatoes, embossed with colored tinselette embossing powder (Enchanted Creations).

3. Party and eyes stamped on white glossy pumpkin die-cut card (all PrintWorks), orange and green color **sponged** in. Layered on green glossy folded notecard. (MA)

4. Invitation done on **computer** with a word-processing program, printed out on glossy cardstock, and cut using the wavy blade of **Fiskars paper cutter.** Leaves adhered with double-stick tape to the printed invitation, and layered on yellow glossy cardstock. (MA)

5. Wrapping paper stamped with leaves colored with markers directly on the rubber before stamping. (NJ)

6. Fabric napkin stamped with leaves using Deka fabric paint, from Hot Potatoes.

7. Thank You Very Much (Love You To Bits) stamped and embossed, and layered on dark red cardstock (PrintWorks). Leaf adhered to cardstock with double-stick foam tape. (NJ)

Birthday Party: (NJ)
All plaid backgrounds (#'s 8, 10, 12) **brayered** with the **"dots, dashes, lines"** technique. Silverware are stamps (by Hot Potatoes) stamped on reverse side of glitter paper and cut out.

8. "Nancy" (NameBrand) stamped with purple marker on separate glossy cardstock, and affixed to **brayered** placecard with double-stick tape, as was the fork. (NJ)

9. Splattered part of Party stamp (Posh) stamped using multi-colored markers, on paper napkin.

10. Invitation stamped (Posh) on glossy white using colored markers. Layered on **brayered** background. with glitter

silverware double-sticked to invitation. (NJ)

11. Glossy gift bag stamped with Happy Birthday (Posh) colored with markers, and splatter added. Yellow **Liquid Applique** added to candle

flame, and "i" in birthday. (NJ)

12. Thanks! (Posh) embossed on brayered, glossy cardstock, cut with wavy scissors and layered on a strip of green construction paper, then pink glossy cardstock. (NJ)

Gotta dance.....

KATIE

Please Join
for
our Fall Festival
Saturday, October
at
The Abel's
Minnetonka, MN 5
RSVP

Happy Birthday!

Party!

Thanks!

PARTY

For-
Date
Time
Place
RSVP

Nancy

Thank Yo
VERY, VERY, VERY MU

High Tech

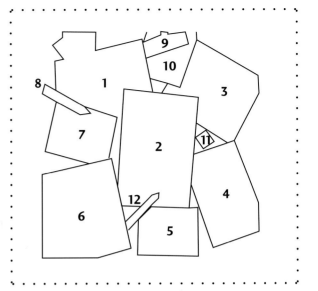

1. **Brayered** background using lagoon Abracadabra rainbow pad. **Postoids**, cancellation stamps, and "postcard" stamped and embossed in black directly on brayered cardstock. Abraham Lincoln is clip art that was **scanned** into a **computer**, printed out, and adhered to the cardstock with double-stick tape. Play money taped behind Lincoln. (CB)

2. Angel scene is clip art copied onto **Drafting Applique film**. All color was **airbrushed** on with the Letrajet airbrush system. "Experience the Joy" (Arizona Stamps, Too) was embossed in gold on the **drafting applique film**. Angels (Hero Arts and Judi-Kins) were embossed in black and colored on separate cardstock, cut out and adhered with double-stick foam tape. Layered on gold holographic paper and black glossy cardstock. (MA)

3. Photo transferred to white glossy cardstock with the **Photo Phinish technique**. A **brayered wash** was applied, using a **paper mask** on center of card. Layered on hot pink construction paper and black glossy cardstock, then layered on glossy cardstock embossed with ìYouíre one in a millionî (PrintWorks) as a **border**, then

layered on silver glitter paper.(MA)

4. Background stamped with a **texture stamp** (PSX) using Abracadabraís rainbow pads. **Postoids** (Stampa Barbara and Judi-Kins) stamped and embossed on separate cardstock, then masked and frogs (Hero Arts) stamped inside. Other postoids embossed and left blank. All adhered with double-stick tape. Additional frogs (ReMaRkable, All Night Media) stamped, embossed, colored, cut out and adhered to blank postoids.(NJ)

5. Background **brayered** with velvet Abracadabra rainbow pad. Sun (TooMuchFun) and dancer (Good Stamps) embossed in black. (CB)

6. Cannibal background scene is **clip art** that was copied onto **Drafting Applique Film** and colored with **colored pencils**. All other images (Rubber Baby Buggy Bumpers and A La Art) were embossed on separate cardstock, colored, cutout and adhered with double-stick foam tape. (MA)

7. All images **hand-carved** by Kandy Lippincott. Colored with markers, layered on white cardstock that was stamped in

orange with a texture stamp, then layered on black cardstock.

8.,12. Tria Marker by Letraset. #8 marker in airhose of **Letrajet airbrush system**.

9. **Brayer**

10. **Abracadabra rainbow pad**

11. **Colorcube** by Niji

Mail Art

1. This beautiful pop-up card was stamped by Cathy Rocca of Chicago using **postoids** and other stamps from Stampa Barbara.

2. **Rubber plunger** sent through the mail (see *Test the Post Office*).

3. Strip of **postoids** done on **computer.** By Pam Sussman for Stampaway convention.

4. Various **mail art** pieces sent and received by many friends.

5. Sheet of **postoids** stamped (Rubber Baby Buggy Bumpers) and **color copied.**

6. Assorted stamped pins (stamped and colored on cardstock, then **laminating sheets** applied, and pin back applied) that are traded by convention-goers at all the conventions.

7. Tag attached to large rubber stamp for mailing. Background is **brayered** using romance Abracadabra rainbow pad. Thanks (Judi-Kins) and stressed woman (Yes! Pigs Can Fly) embossed in black. Mailing label done on sticker paper.

High Tech Stamping

Welcome to the age of home computers, home copiers and other high-tech, fun toys that have found their way into our homes. Whether it's because more of us have home offices, where these machines are a must; or because, as the cost of the machines come down, we are tempted to add them to our ever increasing array of "accessories" to the art world.

Obviously, we did not buy our computer just to play with. Or did we? I actually bought my first computer because it looked like such a fun toy. So, I rationalized all the reasons I HAD to have it...you know, for business, and home accounting, and to reduce the paper I pile up. To my surprise, I ended up using my computer for all the reasons I claimed I needed it for. Except, of course, it didn't seem to reduce my paper piles! But my first love was the fonts and graphics I had to play with. I am definitely a font-junkie. My hard drive is loaded with fonts.

View rubber stamps and computers, and copiers as well, as tools. You can use stamps in conjunction with any other art tools, as well as computers and copiers. There is really no limit to what can be done.

Computers

Using a computer to create art is nothing new. Many fine artists, desktop publishers, and animators use computer-generated art. There are programs from the very simple, easy to use to the complex ones that professional artists manipulate.

The easy ones generally have simpler commands, and perhaps are not as flexible as the higher-end programs. Nevertheless, what can be done is endless. Even most word processing programs have some type of desktop publishing capabilities.

Many rubber stamp companies use computers to typeset words and sayings. Using computer fonts, they are able to get a nice effect, often coming close to the look of hand-calligraphed sayings. With the many fonts available, it is easy to find ones that will fit their needs. Using nothing more than a word processing program, these sayings can be done on the computer and then pasted up and made into rubber. (See the *What Is A Rubber Stamp?* chapter.)

Images are designed on the computer. Clip art can be either bought on disks, or scanned in, and manipulated to the final image. The clip art can be imported into a drawing program. At this point it is easy to add or remove parts of the artwork and rework it.

But, we're not limited to clip art. You can make your own drawings, or rubber stamp a design, then scan it into your computer. Even if you don't have your own scanner, many places, such as Kinko's, will do this for you. Many art schools have provisions as well. Once an image is stored on a disk, it can be used in many computer programs.

With your artwork now on disk, you are able to bring it into a drawing program. You can alter the image, shade it, reverse it. Computers provide incredible ease and speed in creating these images. If you make a mistake, you can just go back to the image you have saved on disk, and start again.

Charles Bandes, of Zum Gali Gali, did the image on the right by combining stamps and computer. He started with a stamped card of patterns and images. Then the design was scanned into the computer, along with a photograph of his eye. In his paint program, the eye image was cut and used as a stamp, repeated across the composition. When everything was positioned as he wanted, an image manipulation program was used to add the fish-eye warped look.

If this seems too complicated, don't be scared off. Using fairly simple programs which include art work, you can combine your stamping with computer play. Two of the most popular computer programs are *Print Artist* (the old *Instant Artist*) and *Print Shop*.

With either of these programs, you can use their clip art to combine with your rubber designs. Use backgrounds, add beautiful sayings, and come up with a pleasing design. Design a border to use with rubber stamps. Make talk and thought bubbles with words to add "talk" to your stamped designs.

CARTOON CHARACTERS STAMPED ON STICKER PAPER AND ADDED TO A DESIGN DONE IN PRINT ARTIST

Print out the design. You may want to copy it onto heavier cardstock, or use a spray adhesive mount and mount it on heavy paper, since most laser papers are fairly lightweight.

You can print your computer artwork out on sticker paper, and sticker the designs to your stamped creations. In this way, you will be able to add computer-aided design elements into your stamped creations.

Once you have your background and art work, bring in your rubber stamped images. Stamp, or stamp and emboss directly

on the print-out. To add more dimension stamp on cardstock, cut it out, and attach it with double-stick tape.

Those who have colored printers can print out the computer-generated designs in color. For those of us with only black and white capabilities, add color after printing. Once the design is printed, treat it as you would a stamped project. Color it in with markers or colored pencils. For a dramatic effect, leave the background black and white, and bring color in with stamped images.

You can design templates on a computer. Many computer drawing programs have envelope and box templates, as well as greeting card and pop-up templates. Or use a draw program to create your own. Print out the template, then adhere it to heavy cardstock. You may be able to run your fancy paper through the computer, right-side down and print the envelope template right on the paper. (All but the slickest paper should accept the toner.) Then just cut and assemble.

Transparency Paper For Lasers

Transparency Paper for Lasers is made to be sent through your laser printer. Use your creativity to combine computer images and stamped images together on transparency paper. Use these in window and frame cards with stained glass images. (For more information, see *Papers*.)

Color

Put color into computer-generated work with foils. There are basically two different types of foils that work with laser printers and copiers. These foils adhere to toner-based images.

▲ Foil, such as CopyFX, can be run through a laser printer.
  • This works for adding spot color to a design. You can highlight words or designs by foiling them in a metallic or bright color.
  • Temporarily adhere the strip of colored foil to the part

of the design you want colored. The foils come with little sticky circles to use for this. Be careful to keep the foil off other parts of the design, as the foil will adhere to any toner-image it covers.

- After the foil is attached to the paper, run it back through the printer. Set your program to print a blank page, as the printer is really heating the foil to bond it.

▲ With Letraset's Color Wand, you can add foil to toner-based designs. The color wand is much like a little iron. Heat it up, and run it over foil that is laid on top of the toner design.

Use computers to design flyers, posters, and newsletters.
Text and stamped designs can be combined easily.

▲ First the newsletter, etc., is designed on the computer.

▲ Images can be stamped to add art and interest to the piece after it is printed out.

▲ If you want the text to flow around designs you are going to eventually stamp, use text frames to block out a portion of the body of the text while working on the computer.

- Most word processing programs, publishing programs, and design programs have the ability to put in a text frame.
- The text frame can be invisible, or you can frame it with a border. It is a block the program inserts, so no text will appear in that space.
- Make your text frame the size of the stamped image you will be adding.

▲ To manipulate stamp images with computer text while working on the computer, stamp the image on acetate.

- With your computer creation on the screen at actual size, you will be able to take the transparency and move it around the screen.
- This will allow you to decide where you want the stamped images. And it will also help you size your text frames.

▲ Use your computer and fancy fonts to make printed invitations. Then add stamping as the design element. (See color photo section.)

Design your own business cards.

▲ Many draw programs and print programs have templates for designing business cards.

▲ You can make up your card, then print them up and cut them to size.

▲ Pre-perforated business card sheets are also available. They can be bought for use with either laser or dot matrix printers.
   ● Combine a computer-designed business card with rubber stamps.
   ● Design the card so that there is a blank space to stamp after the cards are printed.
   ● To make a business card more colorful, add stamped "swooshes" and other background designs on the printed card.

▲ ▲ ▲

Copiers

Copiers can also be used to manipulate art. Playing with the light and dark switch on the copier will change the effect of what you are copying. Copiers can take your art work, in whatever form, and enlarge or decrease it as you need.

Drafting Applique Film

Drafting Applique Film is a self-adhesive backed film, found in art supply stores. It comes in both a matte and clear finish; the matte finish works best for this purpose. It can be used with clip-art along with your stamped designs. Photocopy the clip-art, or whatever you want copied, onto the *drafting applique*,, peel off the back and apply it to your paper or cardstock. You are now able to use it as you would a stamped design. You can embellish the design on the film by coloring with markers or colored pencils, applying glitter, glitter paper, Liquid Applique, or any other add-ons.

The clip-art can be your background or main focus. If you want to stamp and emboss, you can do so directly on the film. Or, stamp images on sticker paper, color, cut and adhere them to your design.

Copy your stamped design, using a very open design such as a vase, onto the drafting applique film. Remove the sticky backing and place on fancy glitzy sticker paper. Cut out the image with the glitter paper and adhere it to your card. You will now have a glittery, patterned, stamped design! (See photo section.)

Transparency Paper for Copiers
Transparency Paper for Copiers also allows a stamped design to be copied onto the transparency. Toner may rub off transparency paper made for lasers because copiers do not get hot enough for these transparencies. It is recommended that you use the right film for the right machine.

▲ ▲ ▲

Although the price on color copiers is coming down slowly, it is still pretty steep for most home offices and craft rooms. However, the price of having color copies made has come down and is very reasonable. When going to a print shop to have something color copied, have a sample copy made first. Not all copiers are alike, and some do not give true colors. Canon copiers and the new Xeroxes are ones to look for.

Rubber stamping and color copies have found their niche together. Color copies offer a nice alternative to stamping many copies of the same thing. It is often very hard to tell a copy from the original.

Color Copiers

Photos, Rubber Stamps and Color Copies

Combine stamping and color photos in color copies for a unique effect. Use the following technique to make unique calendars, photo albums, cards, whatever. You can make as many duplicates as you like from the one original.

▲ Gather photos to use. It could be a year's worth of family activities, one person over a lifetime, or for a specific holiday or birthday card. Maybe you have a very funny photo with an odd mug shot that cries out to be made into a unique card.

▲ If you are making a calendar, you can organize the photos by time of year, holidays, birthday or anniversary for a particular month. Then gather stamps to fit.

▲ Choose stamp images that coordinate with the pictures. Large stamps work the best, as they generally fit with photos easiest. If you don't have a stamp for some part of the picture you're creating, look for images in magazines to cut out and use.

▲ This is good for those photos that didn't come out just perfect. Perhaps you caught someone with a look of surprise on their face, or they appear out of place in the photo. Don't throw these away. You can cut up the pictures and use the parts you need.

▲ For a calendar, plan the design one page at a time:
  • Stamp and color the entire background first.
  • Cut out the parts of the photo you are going to use. Be sure to do a careful job of cutting. Cut out any background that does not apply, and if you're cutting out a person, cut carefully around everything, including each finger, etc.

- Place on the background to see what else might need to be added. Stamp in anything that is needed.

▲ To attach the photos, use double-stick tape to assure they will be firmly adhered.
  - Most of the photos will be taped down directly on the stamped design.
  - For a picture you want coming out of an image, or behind an image, make a slit in the design and slip the photo in from the back. Tape down.
  - If the photo is entirely behind a photoframe, or mirror, etc., cut the center of the design out and tape the photo to the back.

▲ After the photos have all been attached and the design is done, you have your master. It is used to make the color copies (the original shows all the cut lines).

▲ Take the master to a copy shop and have colored copies made. The color copy will not show any cut lines (if you have carefully cut away all unwanted background from your photographic images before putting them on the stamped background). The finished piece will look like the stamping and the photos are all one!

▲ ▲ ▲

The artist postage stamp, also known as "artistamps," has been an important part of Mail Art for over twenty years.

Many faux postage stamps and seals have been made for Mail Art events. You can do the same to commemorate your own events, invent your own worlds, add faces, celebrate heros. Just don't use them in place of real postage!

Faux Postage Stamps

Various ways to make these artistamps:

Postoids

There are rubber stamp designs, available from quite a few stamp companies, called "postoids." These are either empty postal shapes that you can fill as you wish, or clever images of unusual postal stamps. The shapes can be square, rectangle, triangular, oval. There are stamp companies that practically specialize in what are known as postoids.

To use these, you can either:

▲ Stamp them all over envelopes and color them in.

▲ Stamp them with just a colored stamp pad.

▲ Stamp them on sticker paper, cut them out, cutting carefully around their scalloped edge to look like the actual postage stamps. Then stick them on your envelopes.

▲ Make up sheets of postal stamps using the postoids. Stamp them out. You can stamp on sticker paper, or stamp on other paper, and then use an adhesive like *Brush It, Stick It, Lick It* by Enchanted Creations.

There are also blank postoid-design stamps. Add artwork by stamping in designs, using Post-it notes to mask the sides when you stamp. Use your alphabet and number sets to add words and numbers. Or, you can make up your words on a P-Touch by Brother, if you have one. The P-Touch is a little machine that prints out labels. You can get labels that print in black on clear tape, which makes it ideal for paste-ups.

Computer-Aided

Use your computer to design faux postage. Software, such as Print Artist and Print Shop, can be manipulated to create the faux stamp images.

If you want to put any words into the postage, or perhaps numbers, your computer can easily produce these. Try different fonts and different point sizes. Then you will have many sizes to choose from when you make your paste-up.

To make artistamps using Print Artist:
▲   Use the plain business card template.
▲   Border the entire image with a zig-zag border. There are also add-on graphics that have actual postage stamp borders.
▲   Inside the zig-zag, put in a thin line border.
    This will be the basic outline for a postage stamp.
▲   At this point you can go to the print stage, and print out a blank sheet of postal stamps. Or, add your art work right on the screen using the fonts and graphics of the program.
▲   When you are ready, go to "print." The full page will show up on the screen, of one postal stamp. There is a place here to change the percentage of image printed. Making it 50% or 60% will give you a sheet of 48 or so stamps.
▲   When you have what you want, print.
▲   If you have a color printer, you can design in color and print. If not, you will need to add color after printing if desired.

By Copiers
To produce a full sheet of identical stamps, divide an 8 1/2" x 11" sheet to contain as many stamps as possible for the size stamps you are making. Be sure to leave some white space along the margins, and between the stamps.

If you did not use your computer to make the final "paste up" of your faux postage, you will need to do it on a copier. If, for instance you can get 40 stamps to a page, you will have to make 40 copies, cut them out and glue them down. To save time and money, make five copies, paste them up, filling one row across the top. Then have 8 pages of this made up, and paste up the 8 rows together to make a sheet of postoids.

Some copy shops have color copiers that can take your stamp image and produce a full page of stamps. Call around to find someone in your area that can take your finished product, reduce it to the size you want, then repeat it to fill the page. The cost for this should be the cost of one color copy.

You can copy your postoids on sticker sheets to make it easy to adhere the stamps to your envelopes. Gummed papers, found at specialty paper companies, can be used. It is also possible to buy pre-perforated, blank gummed sheets. Some stamp companies and specialty paper companies carry these.

Perforations

The sheet of postage, if not copied on a pre-perforated sheet, needs to be perforated. Perforators are tools that printers use to pierce paper to facilitate separation. There are no inexpensive, true perforators available.

The easiest way to make the perforations is with a pounce wheel, a roller wheel with small metal teeth. Use a cutting mat. Press firmly, with a straight-edge to guide you. Run the wheel along the four sides as well as between the stamps.

You can also use a sewing machine to make your perforations. Run the sewing machine needle (with no thread) along each edge you perforated. To keep your lines straight, put a piece of masking tape along the feed, as a guide for your paper.

If you made your sheet on sticker paper or gummed paper, your stamps are ready to use. For more authenticity, brush *Brush It, Stick It, Lick It*, from Enchanted Creations on the back.

▲ ▲ ▲

Photo Phinish. Suze Weinberg, New Jersey, introduced me to this technique. (See color photo section.)

1. If you are using a colored photo, make sure you use one that has good contrast.
2. Copy the photo to paper on a copier. You may have to make several passes, playing with the settings, until you have a copy with high black and white contrast.
3. Turn the copy upside down on your cardstock Use a color-less blender, such as one by Design Markers, to saturate the back side of the copier paper. A ragged edge will give a look of an old picture, so you do not need to transfer the entire picture if you don't want.
4. As you are running your blender over the paper, lift the edges gently every once in a while and carefully pull off the fibers that may hang between the copy paper and the cardstock.
5. The picture will have transferred onto the cardstock.

HOT TIP

Be sure to use a solvent-based blender. New blenders are now being made with alcohol bases, but these won't work as well. It should say "Zylene solvent base."
CAUTION: This solvent is strong and can eat rubber! Use it in a well-ventilated room.

Besides photos, stamp high contrast black and white scenes, or portrait images. Then send it through a copier and follow the above steps.

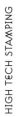

Through the Mail

There are at least two different versions of the term "mail art." The one is a network of "mail artists" communicating with their artwork mainly through the mail. The other encompasses any rubber stamped envelope, card, etc. that is sent by mail. This second use of the term seems to have sprung up with the advent of communications networks, such as Prodigy and Genie. (See *E-Mail* section in this chapter.) It is a much broader use of the term.

For the purposes of this book, I will refer to the original use of the term mail art as Mail Art (capital letters), and anything else as mail art.

Generic mail art is usually done for a specific purpose. It is a "greeting" of some sort...happy birthday, get well, thank you. Mail Art, on the other hand, is just something you want to say, or visual imagery. That is one of the appeals of Mail Art, there is no "reason" for it. It just is. Mail Art is sent to share art with others and it does not matter whether they respond.

Mail Art

Mail Art is also known as *Correspondence Art*. There are probably as many definitions of Mail Art as there are Mail Artists. There are scholarly articles and books on the subject. If you find you are definitely interested, check your nearest library, especially an art school library. This chapter is just to give you a taste of Mail Art, and perhaps whet your appetite for a new way of correspondence and stamp art.

An international network of Mail Artists has been growing over the last 30 years or so. Mail Art was begun by artists who did not believe art should be constrained to the walls of art galleries and museums. Art exhibits, in this sense, take place continually through the mail. It is a very collaborative type of art. The network of Mail Artists are freed from any conventional notions of "art." Anyone can participate. The medium is very flexible.

Mail Art as a movement is an outgrowth of, or parallel to, Fluxist art and Dada art. The early Mail Art people were driven to make a statement about Art. In general, they were unhappy about what had been happening to the art movement. Museum directors and gallery owners were the reigning gurus in Art. The owners were being judgmental. The Mail Artists wanted to do art for art's sake; in a sense they were protesters.

You do not have to be an "artist" to be a "Mail Artist." You just do your "art" and mail it. You, as a Mail Artist, are simply involved in a quirky, fringy, semi-underground activity known as Mail Art.

Mail Art treats Art as an exchange of creativity from one person to another, outside the usual gallery and museum

BEYOND THE BASICS

setting. The Mail Artist would send his art through the mail. The addition of cancellation marks or machine-harm to the art is considered PART of the art itself.

Mail Art is not Mail Art until the Post Office gets a hold of it. Often, art sent through the mail and not protected in any way comes through unscathed. But the postage marks and "distressed mail" one can get is part of Mail Art. The attitude is "Stuff Happens;" that your art won't last for several hundred years, anyway. What you are doing is Process, not so much Product.

Mail Art can be highly political. Many of the people attracted to the movement are feminists or pacifists or animal rights advocates or vegetarians or civil rights activists, etc. Or none, of course. It's a wide open movement.

The essence of Mail Art is that the movement wants ego out of art. Casual exchanges of art fit right in with the re-thinking of one's piece of art. Many Mail Artists who initiate a piece of art ask others to add to it and pass it on. Often the pieces sent out ask the respondent to make additions, or in some way alter the original. They are then instructed to return the work to the sender, or perhaps to send it on to another mail artist who in turn will alter it in some way and send it on.

Mail Art is not just rubber stamp art. Although there is consistent use of rubber stamps in this art, many times it does not include stamping. People in the Mail Art movement do collage, copy machine art, poetry, sketches, sheets of faux postage stamps (see *Faux Postage*), printmaking (including woodblock, litho, eraser carving, etc.), Xeroxing, color copying, faxes, postal stamps, strange gummed stickers, and words or images cut from magazines. You can collage, paint, rubberstamp, sketch, draw, modify other's art.

The words and images are used pictorially, literally, or structurally. Through the use of these words and images Mail Artists produce collages, graphic pieces, poetry and "junk" mail. The purpose can be for aesthetic appeal, as ideas, or satirical.

Mail Art is rarely "cute," unless it is done in a satirical manner; for example, torturing your cute teddy bear. Although Mail Art can be cute, it tends not to be since cute is often not original. It is the mass acceptance of an over-proliferated image. Cute occurs over time. The "60's" images that appear "cute," were not "cute" at the time, but innovative and original ideas that expressed a popular movement. Mail Art is sort of a benign way of making an anti-establishment statement, and creating something visually entertaining at the same time.

If you decide to join in, you will get things you think are wonderful, as well as mail you may consider junk. Mail art is supposed to be judgement free. If you do not like what you get, you need not respond. On the other hand, it does not mean the recipient did not like your mail if you don't receive back. It may be that he/she is too busy to respond right then.

Mail Artists have no OBLIGATION to respond to each other's mail. This is a guilt-free exchange. One does not have to be "timely" in response. There is a total lack of rules. You will get Mail Art only by sending Mail Art. Chances are, you probably will never get back in proportion to what you send. You do not need to send "perfect" work. You can dash something off in a minute. Or spend hours on it.

Mail Art calls can be found listed in both rubber stamp magazines, *Rubberstampmadness* and *National Stampagraphic*. But this is just the tip of the iceberg. Most mail calls are received by Mail Artists through the Mail Art network. Many of the international Mail Artists have never even heard of these magazines. And many Mail Artists do not rubber stamp, so they might not have an interest in that aspect of mail art. When they do stamp, frequently it is with word stamps, many designed in the tradition of some of the stamped "seals" traditionally used in the movement. Sometimes rubber stamps are designed in commemoration of a mail art show.

Once you get involved in Mail Art, more and more Mail Art calls will start showing up in your mailbox. There is a free exchange of Mail Art calls from artist to artist. You pass other's calls for mail art on, they do the same for yours. Many, many forms of art are exchanged. The originator of the mail call will generally produce documentation of all participants, sent to everyone who took part. This is one of the best ways to get yourself known and get in on more mail calls. One mail art call received 600 responses from 27 countries. All those people's names and addresses were included in the documentation. You see that this is a far-reaching, extensive network, and it is very easy to get involved internationally.

Keep in mind that not all Mail Art will meet Sunday School standards. If you are thinking of doing a mail call and plan to show where some might be offended, the words on a Mail Art call "will be displayed in a family setting" or similar words are a sort of code asking for G-rated stuff. The tradition in Mail Art is that everything received is hung. This is a touchy area since the whole tradition of Mail Art is one of complete freedom. Asking Mail Artists to "censor" their art is tricky. But since the movement is such that you can send or not send, reply or not reply, this should not be a problem.

Test the Post Office

Once you get into mailing your art through the post office, you will find that you can send many amazing things. You do not, for example, need to have the address in the lower right-hand corner as we were all taught. Wind the address around the design, incorporate it in the design of the envelope, etc. (This may change, so take advantage of it now.)

You can use the stamp on the envelope to be part of the design. Or, you may just want to pick the perfect stamp for your design. If you have embossed your entire envelope, or in any way made the envelope too slick to keep the stamp stuck, you must do something to adhere it. You can buy self-sticking stamps. Or put a plain piece of sticker paper on the envelope, then put the stamp on the sticker paper. If your envelope is flimsy, or shaped weirdly, you may have the post office hand cancel the stamp so it does not go through the machine.

Besides envelopes and postcards, you can mail just about anything you want through the post office, as long as it is addressed and has the proper postage. For any odd-shaped mail, be prepared to add at least $.10 in additional postage.

I mailed a small rubber plunger to a friend. On the wooden handle, I wrote "If it has a wooden handle, and rubber, it must be a rubber stamp." (I had gotten this idea from Ginny Carter, on Prodigy. See color photo section.) On the rubber I put the address. When I took it to my local post office, I expected an argument, or at least a raised eyebrow from the postal worker. I got neither. He said he'd seen "everything!" You can send letters in plastic soda bottles; put little trinkets in the plastic fish found in gift stores; mail L'Eggs (pantyhose) plastic eggs.

The Great American Stamp Store in Westport, Connecticut put out a mail call "Test the Post Office." They got the most unbelievable things mailed directly: a baby's disposable diaper with a smooshed Snickers bar in it, another diaper with chunky light mustard, a shoe, a cowboy boot from Texas.

▲ ▲ ▲

As computer networks such as Prodigy and Genie began to proliferate, more and more stampers went online. They began to correspond and a new kind of mail art came to be. It can resemble Mail Art in some ways, but has it own look and feel.

To distinguish this from the original Mail Art, this form of mail art is not capitalized in the book. This is for distinction only and not to diminish it in any way.

▲ ▲ ▲

mail art

Rather than Mail Art Calls, most mail art exchanges are called "swaps." Some swaps are more structured than others. Rules can change from swap to swap. The swaps are usually limited, perhaps 10-20 people. A theme is announced: for example, a Valentine swap, a Victorian Fancy swap, a Food swap, etc. Each participant will make the same card for everyone in the swap. A card is either mailed to each of the participating swappers, or all the cards are sent to the swap leader who collates them and sends one of each card to everyone at one time.

mail art swaps

I was lucky enough to be a part of a beautiful swap, and its sequel as well. The swap was called "An Illustrated Poem". "When I Am an Old Lady, I Shall Wear Purple" was the piece picked. Each participant was given a line of the poem. The swap leader had pages all typeset with one line of poem per page. Everyone was mailed enough pages to stamp a page for every participant. Everyone stamped out their pages and returned it to the swap leader. The pages were then spiral-bound and we all received a book. It is a beautiful keepsake of fellow stampers getting together across the country to share a project. I know I will keep mine forever. We now refer to ourselves as the Purple Ladies.

There are long-running swaps as well as one-time ones. They can go on continually for months, or even years, with the same participants. For example, "The Far Side Swap" has been going on for several years. These swaps use The Far Side cartoons as the basis for their monthly exchange. Each person picks a cartoon (from a choice of four), and stamps out their version. There are some very clever works being exchanged.

A "sketchbook," a blank book with a theme, is another type of exchange. The number of blank pages correspond to the number of participants. They can be as large or small as you want. Usually the books are at least 6 pages. Each person who receives the sketchbook stamps out his/her interpretation of a theme on a page, adds their name and address, and sends it on to another stamper who might be interested in participating. The last stamper to fill the book sends it back to the originator, or whoever the book is intended for. It's a nice way to express your own style and see the styles of other stampers.

Still another type of exchange is called a "Slam Book" which has a topic, or question on each page. Every person who gets the book stamps once on each page according to the subject at the top of each page. An example would be "Stamp something you would find in the park."

Swaps are a great way to see a lot of different styles of stamping, correspond with people you would otherwise not have met, and make some wonderful new friends. Each swap piques your interest to see more and different styles. It is a great way to add to your stamping repertoire and learn new techniques.

▲ ▲ ▲

When you join a swap, you may want some sort of system to keep track of your project and a way to store the wonderful stamped works you'll receive. There are many ideas for doing this. The following are a few ways that swappers have suggested. You may like one of these ideas, or you may find a new way that suits you.

▲ If you joined a swap on a bulletin board, print out a list of participants. Fold in half and put in a 6"x9" *Kraft envelope*. Write in large marker the name of the swap and date. As each card comes in, check off the name of the sender and put the card in the envelope. Or, make a pocket using the print-out folded in half (with the names on the outside) and stapled.

▲ Use a *folder with pockets* on each side. The right side has the print-outs from the swaps you're in, in the order they're due. As one is finished, the print-out is moved to the left side. Mark the lists as you receive cards.

Suggestions for storing the artwork you receive:
▲ Keep swap cards in plastic sleeves in 3-ring binders. The 5"x7" sleeves work for most cards, and the full-page sleeves for larger pieces. Keep the cards in place in these plastic sleeves by using temporary dry-line adhesive.
▲ Giant photo albums with peel off plastic sheets are good for keeping cards. The page inside the plastic covering is sticky and holds the cards in place, while the plastic covering protects them. The albums are 3-ring binders, so you can add more sheets.
▲ Use a recipe file box to keep track of all mail art sent and received. Everyone who has sent mail art, or received mail art from you, will have a card with name and address.
▲ Update the cards with the date and name of the swap, or a description of the card. Mark it "S"(sent), or "R"(received), or both for swaps.

Make Your Own Envelopes

Add interest to mailings with unusual envelopes. This serves as both a decorative touch, and is practical, as well, if you need a special-sized envelope.

The use of templates and using unusual materials was covered in my book, **The Art of Rubber Stamping, Easy as 1, 2, 3**. Besides the templates that you can make (see *High Tech* chapter), and templates you can buy from rubber stamp and stencil companies, there are many fun folding techniques for simple but unique envelopes.

I've included three very simple folded envelopes. The first is a very practical technique to know. It will come in handy for all those cards that will not fit into any normal-sized envelopes. The other two are unique, fun envelopes that are simple to do once you get the basic folding technique. Use fun papers with these envelopes, such as origami papers, magazine pages, and all your handmade and hand-dyed papers.

The Simple Fold #1:

1. Use a sheet of decorative paper large enough to hold your stamped card.
2. Place your card on the paper,
3. Fold sides A and B along the sides of the artwork so they overlap each other. Secure with double-stick tape.
4. Fold up the bottom, C. Round the edges before folding for a more finished look. Secure with double-stick tape.
5. Round off the upper corners of D. Fold down.
6. For the flap:
   ▲ *Brush It, Lick It, And Stick It,* by Enchanted Creations, is a re-moistenable glue. Made for envelope flaps, but can make your own stickers, etc. It even comes in flavors!
   ▲ Use UHU stick glue. Apply the glue to the flap of the envelope. Leave it open to dry. When ready to use, lick and stick just like a purchased envelope. UHU can be found at most office supply and stationery stores.
   ▲ Make your own envelope glue. Mix 3 parts Elmer's glue to one part vinegar. Mix well and let dry. *Don't lick it.*
   ▲ Wet it with a sponge to wet and close.
   ▲ You can use double-stick tape once you have put in your card.

FIGURE 1

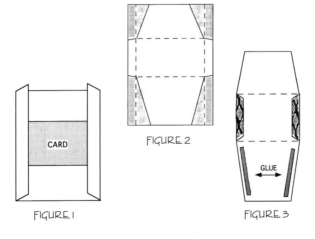

FIGURE 2

FIGURE 3

Folded Envelope #2

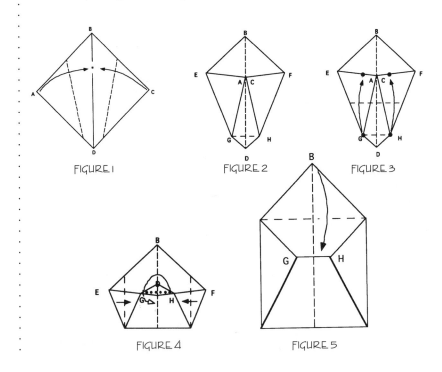

1. Use a square piece of paper, any size.
2. Make a light crease diagonally, BD.
3. Fold the corners, A and C, to the crease. Do not let them fold all the way to D.
4. Make a crease G to H. Unfold.
5. Fold up the bottom, D, so that the GH crease lies on the edges of AE and CF.
6. Fold D inside, on GH crease. This will lock in GH.
7. Fold in E and F, butting them against the edges going up to GH.
8. Make a crease from E to F. Slide point B under the GH edge.
9. There you have an envelope that stays together with no glue. Describing it is harder than the folding! This is really a very simple envelope to make.

FIGURE 1

FIGURE 2

FIGURE 3

FIGURE 4

FIGURE 5

1. Use a square piece of paper, any size. This looks especially nice with 2-sided origami paper.
2. Fold a diagonal crease lightly in one direction, A to B.
3. Open and fold diagonally in the other direction lightly, C to D.
4. Open. Fold D up to the center mark. Smooth this crease firmly.
5. Fold again on the original AB diagonal line. Crease firmly.
6. Divide this triangle into 3 vertical parts, WX and YZ.
7. Fold WX over to the right. Fold YZ to the left. Crease both folds firmly.
8. Fold front point back to meet left-hand fold.
9. This will form a triangle. Open up this triangle so that it forms a rectangle.
10. Fold B down, and tuck it into the rectangle.
11. Although no glue is needed for this envelope, it does not lock shut like #2. You may want to stick it closed, or otherwise adhere it.

Japanese Folded Envelope #3

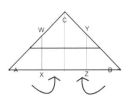
FIGURE 1

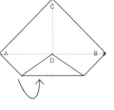
FIGURE 2

FIGURE 3

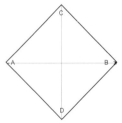

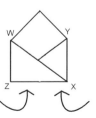
FIGURE 4

FIGURE 5

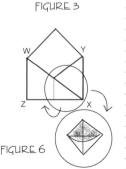
FIGURE 6

E-Mail and Other On-Line Fun

Do you feel all alone in the middle of rubber wasteland, where there are few, if any, stamp stores? Are there no other stampers you can communicate and stamp with? Does no one understand your addiction to rubber?

Join the information highway. All you need is a modem connected to your computer, and membership on one or more of the on-line services. These services all have rubber stamping groups found on "bulletin boards."

Most have a monthly fee, and an hourly charge for use. If you do not live in an area with a local access number, you may have to pay a charge for the telephone usage as well. Although this sounds like an expensive hobby, there are ways to keep costs down. Some have off-line ways of communicating. (You read and reply to the "posts" while not connected, and use the modem and network time just to download your information.)

Genie, Prodigy, America Online, People Together, and Compuserve are a few of the services.

America OnLine	800-827-6364
Compuserve	800-848-8199
Genie	800-638-9636
People Together	510-548-1516
Prodigy	800-776-3449

This is the place to share ideas and ask questions. With people from all over the country always experimenting with new techniques, you are on the cutting edge of rubber.

Most stampers who join an electronic bulletin board take "rubber names." My rubber name is Sparkle Plenty. My favorite name is "*THE RUBBER FAIRY*," because I loved her reasoning. When asked why she choose that name, Diana Langhauser replied:

"My name comes from having to 'hide' those stamp purchases from my husband! You know what I mean, when your collection increases by 15 stamps overnight and you can't explain it. Well, that's because you've had a visit from.......
......the rubber fairy!"

There are swaps you can join on-line; often up to 30 different ones at any time. When you are in a swap, you will see many different styles of stamping. A themed swap will allow you to see other's interpretations of the same subject and each card will be unique.

You can learn about rubber stamp conventions, held across the country. If you can't make a convention, there is always a lot of talk afterwards on what went on at the convention. When you go to a convention, you will feel like you are meeting old friends. There are often plans to meet somewhere during the convention. All the "names" you have been communicating with will come alive! All your new friends will be there. You will then find what you have already discovered: Rubber stampers are warm, sharing people.

What is a Rubber Stamp?

Up until now we have been taking the term "rubber stamp" for granted. But what is a rubber stamp? And how is it made?

A good rubber stamp has 3 parts.
1. **The die:** the rubber that takes the ink and makes the impression.
2. **The cushion:** the padded part between the die and the wood handle.
3. **The mount:** the wooden part the cushion is attached to. **The index** is the image of the design on the wood handle.

WOOD MOUNT   INDEX

CUSHION

RUBBER DIE

A rubber stamp starts out as a design. The design can be hand-drawn, computer designed, calligraphic writing, clip art*, or any other method to get the design on paper.

F O O T

N O T E

*Clip art is copyright-free art often found in books such as Dover Publications. Many stamp companies take this clip art and "redo" it in some way to make it their own... such as deleting or adding to the design, or in some way making a change. The companies that redo a clip art image now claim the new design as their own. The original design itself, however, is in the public domain and can be used by others.

Designs that are done as original art work for the stamp companies carry a copyright protection, and cannot be copied in commercial form. Rubber stamps are sold with the understanding that the image is being used in a personal, non-commercial way, and will be hand-stamped. If you wish to use stamps in any other way, you must get the permission of the individual stamp company. Every company varies on the way it allows the use of their designs.

▲ ▲ ▲

The Making of a Rubber Stamp

PASTE-UP BOARD

The process of making a rubber stamp begins with the initial design. The design, or generally many designs, are pasted up on an "artboard," such as poster board, to make it camera-ready. The size of the paste-up varies by the size of the vulcanizer that will be used to produce the rubber. Generally, they run about 5" x 7" to 9" x 11".

First, make photocopies of the designs you want. Do the touch-up work on the copies. You want nice, clean lines with no smudging, as every speck of black or gray will show up on the finished die. Paste up the designs on an artboard, such as posterboard, using rubber cement or temporary spray mount. With this type of adhesive, it is easy to pick up the designs and re-position them as you want them.

HOT TIP

If you use rubber cement, get a rubber cement "pick up" at an art store. It will remove the excess cement from the artboard. Remember, it is important that the artboard be as clean as possible.

The artboard is sent to a printer who will make a negative of the drawing. The negative is sent to an engraver and an engraved, ridgelon plate is made. This is used to make a matrix board in the vulcanizer. The plate is then put aside and saved.

A sheet of rubber is placed on top of the matrix board, and both are pressed together between two metal plates in the vulcanizer at about 315°. The rubber oozes into the depressions in the matrix and within 6-10 minutes becomes vulcanized. The rubber is cooled, removed from the board, and the images cut to be mounted. The matrix can be used over many times.

A few stamp companies have the equipment necessary to complete all the steps in making the rubber. Others need to farm out some of the steps. And some companies pay other stamp manufacturers to make their stamps for them.

Stamps purchased from stamp companies are generally mounted on fine maple blocks of wood, which have been cut, sanded and indexed. The indexing, the image on top of the mount, is that of the rubber design. Indexing is done with permanent ink, or pigment ink, directly on the wood. Or the design is copied, either in black and white, or in color, on transparent film and adhered to the top of the mount.

When you buy a stamp from a stamp company, there are certain things you should expect to find.
▲ The rubber itself (the die) should be trimmed carefully and closely.
▲ There should be a layer of cushion between the rubber and the wood. The cushion should be cut carefully and closely as well.
▲ The indexing should be placed on the mount in the same position as the rubber image on the reverse. This will allow you the ability to line up your design when you stamp.

Most stamps you buy are mounted on wood. They make the easiest, nicest way of using rubber stamps. However, to save money to the consumer, many stamp companies will make sets in which the rubber is mounted on a cushion only. Although these are not always as easy to use, nor do they always make as good impressions (often the rubber edges leave ink marks), there are some well-made rubber sets. I prefer the sets with

the very thick cushion, and deep-etched rubber. With these, the choice is often just aesthetics.

▲ ▲ ▲

Rubber Problems (and Solutions)

Problem: A stamp that leaves an "extra" image when stamped.

Solutions:

▲ Use markers, rather than an ink pad, to color the stamp.
▲ Then you only need to ink the image, carefully avoiding any "trouble spots."
▲ Perform "surgery" on the rubber die. It is not too hard to cut away the excess rubber.
  • Before you cut, stamp the image a few times on paper.
  • Look at the stamped design to figure out where the offending rubber is. This will also give you an idea of how much you need to remove.

HOT TIP

Remember, as you're looking at your paper, the rubber you look at is in reverse! So, if there is a mark along the right side of your design when stamped, the rubber you will be cutting away is on the left as you look at it.

  • Use a sharp X-Acto knife. Push down into the rubber, angled slightly away from the raised design edge. (You want the knife angled away, so as not to undercut the design. Undercutting leaves the rubber image with inadequate support.)
  • Cut carefully through the rubber, then gently using the tip of the blade, lift off the excess rubber. You can either cut off the cushion as well, or leave it.
  • Take the rubber and cushion completely off the wood mount before cutting. Trim the rubber and cushion, then re-mount.
  • You can only do this if it is not on double-stick mounting cushion. Do not force.

▲ ▲ ▲

Problem: A stamp design with a large "negative" space inside the design leaves a shadow. Negative space refers to the space inside large stamps that should not print, such as the inside of a frame design, a tv, a fishbowl, an empty vase, etc.

Solution:

▲ You can cut out the "negative spaces" as well as the rubber around the image.
   • Cut out the entire blank middle of the design and remove, carefully cutting slightly away from the raised image.
   • Be careful not to cut into the design. (See above.)
▲ Or, use markers to ink up the image, to avoid getting ink in the middle of the design.

▲ ▲ ▲

Problem: Your stamp sets that are only mounted on cushion do not stamp easily or well.

Solution:

▲ Pull the rubber off the cushion, and follow the instructions for mounting stamps that follows.
▲ Or, mount the whole thing (stamp and cushion) on a wood block. This will make them easier to use.

Mounting Your Own Stamps

RUBBER DIE

You can buy "unmounted" stamps from some stamp companies and mount them yourself. Companies that sell unmounteds usually charge about half the retail price of the stamp. Many companies sell grab bags of unmounted stamps for a set price, generally less than individual unmounteds. Some grab bags are better than others, depending on the company (and, of course, on luck!).

CUSHION

There are stamp companies that sell cushion and wood as well as their dies; other companies specialize in just the supplies. Or, you can make your own mounts:

▲ Get strips of wood from lumber yards, and cut to the size you need.

▲ Also, look for inexpensive, small mounts:

WOOD MOUNT
TOP

- "Cedar nuggets," found in stores that sell household items, will work as small blocks for small dies.

- For very small unmounted dies, you can trim them and use double stick tape to mount them on a small acrylic box (such as a Tic-Tac box).

- To save on buying a lot of wood, especially for designs you won't use that often, put a piece of velcro on the rubber die. Put another piece of velcro on a wood mount. Use the 'velcroed' mount for many rubber dies.

- Have different wood sizes with velcro. Dies that are all approximately the same size can use the same mount. Mount on double-stick tape, and stick on a wood mount, for temporary use.

HOT TIP

When you trim your rubber, save all the little pieces of rubber that you usually throw away. Then mount them on wood to make a "texture" type of background stamp.

You will need:
- ▲ Cushion
- ▲ Rubber cement (for non-adhesive cushion)
- ▲ Wood mounts
- ▲ Pigment or permanent ink, or stick paper

1. Mount the rubber dies on cushion.

For double-sided self-adhesive cushion *:
- ▲ Pull the backing paper off the first side of the cushion, and place the dies on it.
- ▲ Position the dies as close to each other as you can to save cushion. Be sure to leave enough space between them to be able to cut around each one.

For non-adhesive cushion *:
- ▲ Use rubber-cement for gluing the rubber to the cushion.
- ▲ Be sure to work in a well-ventilated area.
- ▲ Spread the cement onto the rubber, and onto the cushion.
- ▲ Let it dry tacky.
- ▲ When dry, stick the image onto the cushion.
- ▲ Again, position the dies as close as possible to save cushion, allowing enough room to cut between each one.

F O O T

N O T E

* These cushions can be bought from some stamp companies, and companies that sell mounting supplies. Other alternatives for cushions are:
- *Dr. Scholl's foot pads.*
- *Inexpensive foam-backed placemats.*
- *Knee cushions (used in gardening).*
- *Fun Foam (thin sheets like the foam tub toys).*

Cut the rubber die and the cushion as closely as possible. Be careful not to cut through the design, and do not undercut the rubber. Keep your X-Acto or scissors at a slight angle away from the design.

To Mount

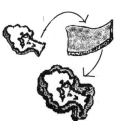

MOUNT RUBBER DIE

TO CUSHION

Select the right size wood mount for your die. The wood mount should not be smaller than the rubber. But, it only needs to be a small fraction larger than the die all the way around. If it is too large, the wood can pick up ink from the stamp pad, and stamp the extra ink on your paper, just as extra rubber can.

2. Index the wood mount.

To index your stamps:

▲ Stamp the image on the wood, with pigment or permanent ink. If you stamp with the pigment ink, you can also emboss the image, but it is not necessary.

▲ Or, copy the design on self-stick transparency paper, cut and stick to the wood top.

TOP OF STAMP

RUBBER
DIE ON
CUSHION

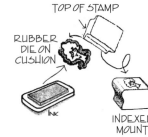

INK

INDEXED
MOUNT

To index by stamping on the wood directly, do this before you mount the rubber die and cushion to the wood.

▲ Lay the rubber die, adhered to cushion, face up on the table.

▲ Ink it with either pigment or permanent ink.

▲ Carefully press the top of the mount down onto the inked rubber. (Some mounts have a definite top and bottom. The bottom side where the die is attached is usually flatter.)

▲ Make sure to make a good impression.

HOT

TIP

To do a really nice job, first lay the wood mount on a piece of paper and trace around the perimeter with a pencil. Now take your die, ink it and position it image-side up within the pencilled outline you just drew. Lower the wood mount, guiding it to the pencil lines to direct the positioning of the indexing. Make sure you press hard, and cleanly, to make a good impression.

▲ Let the ink dry.

▲ When the ink is dry, seal the wood.
  • Spray the wood with a clear matte acrylic coating.
  • Or coat with clear nail polish.

HOT TIP

If the ink bleeds on your wood when you are stamping the image, spray the wood first with the acrylic coating. This will "fix" the wood. Let it dry. Then stamp the image. Let dry, and spray again to coat the image.

▲ If you use permanent black ink, the ink should not bleed.
  • Put permanent ink on a blank stamp pad.
  • You will need to re-ink the pad often, as permanent ink dries out faster than water-based ink.
  • Clean-up for permanent ink is not a problem if you do it immediately after stamping. Use denatured alcohol in a scrubby-topped bottle.
▲ You can use clear, sticky-back copy film before or after you attach the rubber die and cushion to the wood mount.
  • Stamp out all the stamp images in black on a white sheet of paper.
  • Copy it on self-sticking transparency paper.
  • Cut out, and stick on the top of the wood mount, rather than stamping the image.
▲ You can stamp the image on white sticker paper after the stamp has been mounted. Put the sticker on top of the wood mount for an index. Seal with a clear piece of packing tape.

3. Mount the rubber die and cushion onto the indexed wood mount.
For the double-sided self-stick cushion,
  • Remove the backing off the cushion which is affixed to the die.
  • Press this to the middle of the wood mount.
  • If the mount has already been indexed and sealed, that is it.....you now have a rubber stamp!
For rubber cushion,
  • Spread a layer of contact cement or rubber cement to the back of the cushion, and another layer to the wood mount.

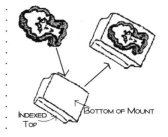

INDEXED TOP   BOTTOM OF MOUNT

- Let them both dry to a tacky finish. Now stick the two together... Voila! your rubber stamp.

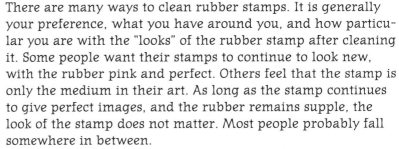

Cleaning Stamps

There are many ways to clean rubber stamps. It is generally your preference, what you have around you, and how particular you are with the "looks" of the rubber stamp after cleaning it. Some people want their stamps to continue to look new, with the rubber pink and perfect. Others feel that the stamp is only the medium in their art. As long as the stamp continues to give perfect images, and the rubber remains supple, the look of the stamp does not matter. Most people probably fall somewhere in between.

Cleaning solutions that can be used:
▲ Commercial stamp cleaners.
  - These generally come in roll-top applicators.
  - Roll it over the stamp, then pat dry on a towel.
  - Judi-Kins makes a conditioning cleaner that contains glycerin.
▲ Other cleaning solutions to use on stamps.
  - Plain water, or mixed with some dish detergent.
  - Windex (without ammonia), either straight or diluted half-and-half with water.

Ways to use the cleaners:
- Scrub stamp with stamp cleaner that comes in a scrub-top bottle, then blot on a towel.
- Spray Windex on paper towel, then blot on stamp.
- Use a small plastic tray or a foam tray. The little trays from microwave meals work great. Soak a paper towel with a cleaning solution in the tray. Have another tray with a dry paper towel. Stamp on the damp towel to remove the ink, then stamp on the other to dry the stamp.

- Use a fuzzy replacement-pad paint edger found in hardware and paint stores.
- Put the pad on a small plastic tray and soak in cleaning solution.
- Twist the stamp on the edger. Then dry. The bristles get in the crevices of the stamp and rid it of ink.

T A K E

N O T E

Warning: For those who like a pristine-clean stamp, these fuzzy pads may stain the bottom of the wood mount!

▲ Baby wipes that come in flat, shallow containers work well.
- Flip the lid open and stamp your dirty stamp on the top wipe.
- When that one gets too dirty, peel it off, throw it out, and use the next one.
- Blot the stamp on a dry rag or paper towel to dry. Or rub the stamp over a dry fuzzy pad.
- Look for baby wipes that contain no alcohol.

▲ ▲ ▲

Renewing Stamps

Rubber stamps that have been mistreated, or have become old, hard, or "funky," can often be renewed and regenerated. If the rubber on a stamp is very hard, or won't take ink, it can be because it has been exposed to sunlight. Or it may have been cleaned too many times with a drying-type of a cleaner.

There are several things that can be done that will hopefully renew the rubber to its original state.
▲ A good scrub may be all that is needed.
▲ Leave the stamp, rubber side down, on paper towels moistened with stamp cleaner.

Rub a pencil eraser over the rubber to take off unknown residue.
Go over the rubber with very fine sandpaper.

▲ ▲ ▲

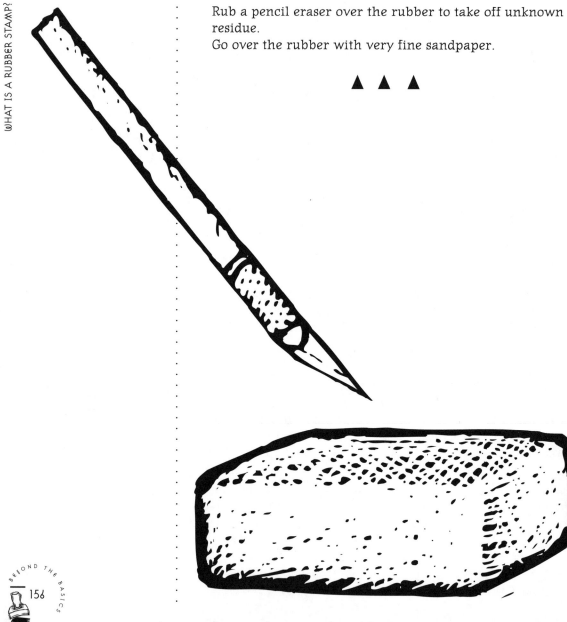

Carving Your Own

The rewards of carving an eraser are immediate. You can design, carve, and then stamp the image instantly upon completion. This can give a very satisfying feeling of accomplishment.

There is a delight in having a design you have made yourself. You do not need to be able to draw in order to carve. It is easy to find a picture of what you need and transfer it to an eraser and carve. All you need are some basic tools and a little knowledge. The more you carve, the more you will learn.

You need:
▲ Erasers.
- Most carvers prefer the Staedtler Mars Plastic Grand eraser, which can be found in art stores. They are 1 1/2" x 2".
- Nasco makes a product called Safety-Kut which comes in many sizes, so you can carve larger projects. It is less expensive than the Staedtler Mars eraser.

▲ Linoleum block cutter handles. Hunt/Speedball has one that has a short, fat orange handle. Another Lino Cutter Handle, available through Nasco, is long and pen-like. I prefer this one, as I find it easier to control.
▲ Blades, known as lino cutters. Depending on the size, there are liners and gouges. The majority of your carving will be with the #1 liner, but you will want a u-shaped gouge as well.

▲ X-Acto knife.
▲ *Non-oily*, acetone nail polish remover.
▲ Cotton balls.
▲ Soft rag.
▲ Photocopied design, or a design from a newspaper.
▲ Soft pencil.

First, you need to create or select an image to carve. It can be a hand-drawn design, clip-art, or a design found in a newspaper. Anything can be carved, but if you are a novice, begin with something simple.

Transferring the image to the eraser:

▲ If you are using the Mars Staedtler eraser, use cotton balls dipped in the nail polish remover to wipe off the black printing on the eraser.

▲ Or, photocopy the design you want to carve. The photocopy makes it easy to transfer the design. (With a design from a newspaper, you can use the acetone without photocopying first.)

▲ If the design is hand-drawn with pencil, or directly from a "fresh" newspaper, just turn it upside down on the eraser and rub it with your finger to transfer.

HOT TIP

Since you are going to turn this upside down to transfer, make sure your design will be going the direction you want. This is especially important with words.

▲ Place the photocopy face down on the eraser, keeping it firmly in place.

▲ Dampen a cotton ball with the acetone nail polish remover and rub it over the paper.

▲ Peel the paper off the eraser. There should be a clear copy of the design.

• If it all hasn't transferred, put the paper back down and carefully redo the incomplete section only.

• If you make a mess of it, just use the dampened cotton ball to remove the whole thing and start again.

▲ You can also transfer a hand-drawn design directly onto the eraser.

- Trace your eraser onto vellum (or tracing paper), so you have the size of the eraser.
- Using a soft pencil, lightly draw or trace on vellum the image you want carved within the outline of the eraser.
- Place this drawing on a flat, hard surface.
- Put the eraser on top, and firmly press with a steady firmness. Be careful not to jiggle the eraser, as the design will smear.

To carve:

▲ Put your eraser on a piece of cardstock so that you can rotate it easily as you carve.

▲ Using the linoleum cutter, remove the parts of the eraser that are not part of the design. You will be cutting away the white parts of the eraser, leaving the black of the design.

▲ Use the smallest blade of the linoleum cutter for most of the cutting, although the larger blades are good for scooping out large white areas.

▲ Do not undercut the eraser. The blade should be angled away from the line. (See *Mounting*.)

▲ Carve carefully.

▲ When you think your design is finished, blow off the loose carving crumbs. Ink up the design and stamp it.

▲ Examine the print you just made to determine where you might need to clean up the carved image.

▲ You will rarely have a perfect image the first time. Just keep working with it. And keep stamping and checking.

▲ Once you are happy with your print, you are done! Wash off the eraser carefully to remove any ink and polish residue.

Tips on handling the carving tool:

▲ You will get variety in the looks of your carving by the way you cut with your tools.

▲ Carving is a skilled craft that comes with practice, so don't let yourself get easily discouraged.

▲ Use a piece of cardstock under your rubber as you carve. This will allow the block to turn and change direction when you want it to.

▲ Start with the small v-tip. Dig into the space beside the line of the image just a little. Then PUSH with the blade away from you just under the surface.

▲ Keep the blade shallow.

▲ Practice to get a steady depth.

▲ When you get to the end of your stroke, lift the tool. Brush across the eraser bit to tear it free.

▲ When you are carving towards a black design line, stop short of the line so you don't cut through.

▲ Don't go too slow, as your hand will wobble.

▲ For a zig-zag line, hold your tool like a pencil. Twirl the blade back and forth.

▲ To get cross-hatching, a needle will work well.

▲ To make round holes: straight pins will make small holes, the end of a paper clip will make larger ones.

▲ Use both hands to get a smooth, curved line. While carving with your one hand, use your other to spin the carving block around by turning the piece of cardstock it's sitting on.

I have just given you some of the very basics for learning to carve erasers. For more information, look for back issues of *Rubberstampmadness* (and I'm sure more to come), as well as books on the subject. And look into *Eraser Carver's Quarterly*, a "zine" especially for carving enthusiasts.

Storage

There seems to be a universal problem among rubber stamp artists and collectors. It starts when we buy a couple of stamps, an ink pad, and maybe some markers.

We come up with ways of keeping our products together.

There is the shoe box...the cardboard discarded one, then the nice plastic one.

Soon that gets overcrowded, so next comes the handled, plastic tote, perhaps.

Or maybe you jump directly to the tool box or fishing tackle box. That seems to be the perfect solution. The little trays pop up and out. There is enough room for stamps on the trays, and accessories on the bottom. And it's so handy. Just pick it up by its nice carrying handle and take it to your stamping table.

We start to discover unusual papers to stamp on, and to layer with.

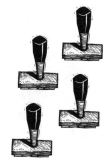

We add some more accessories.

We need a heat gun, a paper cutter, and a mini-paper cutter.

A stamp positioner and paper for it, masks and Post-its, more ink pads.

More markers.

New embossing powders, new colors.

And meanwhile, the number of stamps keeps growing.

So what is the solution for this ever-growing monster that has taken over our houses, all our storage space, uses our dining rooms, family rooms, spare rooms, kitchens, etc.?

There is no one perfect solution for everyone. But there are lots of ideas for you to use, adapt to your situation, and change as you need to. That's probably the most important word with this fascinating new hobby, art and craft: **CHANGE!**

The only thing I can guarantee is that you will always need more room, different room, different ways to store. So when you pass that shoe box stage, you are going to be set adrift on a sea of never-ending choices and ever-changing needs. Begin by looking at what you have, what you like and what you need. Keep one thing in mind: don't plan to get a container, or containers, that will perfectly hold what you own right now. Think of this as building a house for a small family that will grow ...your kids multiply, and they get bigger, and they bring home friends, and stray pets begin to appear at your doorstep, and they bring more with them, and they get bigger!

Whenever you buy storage, always buy bigger than you think you need. Or buy containers that can be added to, expanded, or combined.

I could open a used container store to sell everything I have outgrown! One nice thing about all these boxes and storage units is I can often take an old, small box and use it to divide up a group of items. So I have my own selection of containers downstairs just waiting to be used again!

Storing Stamps

After emerging from the shoe boxes and the handy-dandy carrying tote, you will probably find that the number of your stamps are growing, and just dumping them all together is not the easiest way to find what you need when you want to stamp.

The first step is to begin by making broad categories. These can be broken down into smaller groups later.

For example, you might want to take all your animal stamps and put them together. As your stamps grow, you may need to break these down again: dogs and cats, small animals, wild animals, amphibians, birds, etc.

The same for scene stamps: they can later be broken down by outside, inside, floral, summer, winter, etc.

Ways to store stamps by category:
▲ Plastic shoe boxes for each category.
▲ Buy stackable letter trays you find in office supply stores.
- You can often get a package of 3-6 for a reasonable price.
- They can stack as high as you have room for them.
- Use acrylic box frames from a discount store, a size that will fit the letter trays, usually 8" x 10", Use 1 box frame per stackable tray.
- Each tray will hold one category. Therefore, you could begin by having a tray with a box frame that holds your animal stamps. As your collection grows, you can

Categorize your stamps

add more trays, more frames, and keep separating out your stamp categories.

- This is an exceptionally handy, very flexible way to store your stamps.
- I use masking tape with the name of the category on the lucite frame, so I know what is stored in each tray just by looking.
- These letter trays are also good for holding the paper you use.

▲ Pizza boxes, or hinged boxes. You can stamp the image of the stamps you keep in that box on the cover, so you know what is in each box without having to open it.

▲ Roll around carts with drawers.

▲ Plastic containers that have from one to six individual drawers, can be found in discount stores and craft stores.

▲ Tool chests with drawers.

▲ Shelves on the walls or free-standing shelving. The shelves needn't be very deep for the stamps. The narrower the shelf, the easier to see your stamps.

▲ If you are lucky enough to find cast-offs, look for library card catalog chests, optometrist drawers, dentist files.

▲ The Elfa drawer system that I talked about in my first book is still my favorite way of holding my stamps.

- This system is more expensive than the stacking file trays; however, the drawers can be bought much wider, so you will get more in each drawer.
- These units can be added on: stacked on top of each other, or next to each other.
- With several units, you can suspend a top over the drawers, leaving a space to sit. This will give you a place to work right by your stamps!!

Storing
the
Accessories

Besides stamps, you now will have a pretty good collection of accessories you need to store.

Stamp Pads

There is more to consider than just where to put your stamp pads. Different types of inks need different storage considerations.

When storing your stamps, do not forget:
▲ *Non-pigment*, felt ink pads should be stored upside down.
▲ However, do NOT store *pigment* ink pads upside-down.
▲ Rainbow pads should *never* be stored on their sides.
   (see section on *Inks* for more information)

Okay, so where can you store these?
▲ If your collection is large enough, you can choose to get a tape cassette rack, and store each pad in a slot.
▲ Or buy small bins and put certain colors together: darks, primary, pastels, rainbows, pigment, etc.

There are also the Inkits, Colorcubes, and Cat's Eyes.
▲ These are small square or oval-shaped pigment ink pads.
▲ The color comes on a sponge surface that is raised above the lip of the holder and can be sponged on any size stamp.

▲ They are less expensive than the full-sized pigment pads which allows you to have a nice selection of colors.

▲ Store them together to see your assortment.
  • Keep them together in a bin.
  • Use a plastic, divided "floss box". It has a flip-top lid, with little compartments, made for storing embroidery floss. Found in craft and sewing supply stores, they are the perfect size to hold the little cubes.

H O T

T I P

These floss boxes can also be used to keep your small mounted alphabets.

Markers

Your collection of markers, pencils, watercolors, etc. also need to be stored together in a handy place.

The best way to store markers is upside down, straight up. With the double-sided pens, store them lying flat. (I am not careful in storing *my* pens upside down, and they seem to live for a long time anyway!)

I keep my pens and pencils in plastic drinking cups. All my fat Marvy's in one cup, another cup for my thinner markers, one for my Tombow pens, and another that holds my water-color pencils and a small watercolor brush.

I also have a cup to hold:
▲ an X-Acto knife
▲ a scoring tool
▲ a long tweezers (for picking up small stones and collage items to place on my work)
▲ a glue stick
▲ a black felt writing pen
▲ embossing pens of different sizes

▲ a scissors

If you prefer your pens and pencils laying flat, a divided box with long narrow drawers will work really well. Each drawer can hold different types of markers and pencils.

There are also acrylic pen holders sold at some stamp stores specifically for markers. These holders are angled, and have 20-40 holes drilled into the holder to accomodate the fat Marvy markers. The most convenient way to use these holders is to glue the cap into the hole. (Even when you need to re-place a dry marker, you can use the old cap!) When you need a color, pull out the marker, and the cap stays in place.

Embossing Powders
▲ Store the small bottles of embossing powders in a drawer or drawers (depending on how many colors and types you have).
▲ Use a lazy Susan for all your bottles of embossing powder.
▲ If you tend to emboss a lot, or if you emboss with one particular powder a lot, consider a larger holder. Pour a couple of bottles of the same powder into a container. You will want something that is large enough for you to dip an average size card into the container, under the powder, and back out. In this way, there will be very little mess—it will be contained in the holder—and there will be no waste of unused powder.
▲ Good holders for this purpose:
  • The square Rubbermaid sandwich containers found at discount stores are a perfect size.
  • A plastic or acrylic jewelry chest with 3-4 card-sized drawers can hold different colored powders and/or glitter in each drawer.

Odds and Ends
There are always small pieces of "things" we may need: bottles

of confetti, bags of mylar shred, sticky jewels, stickers, ribbons, raffia, punches, etc.

▲ Keep them in a plastic shoe box, or chests with small drawers (you remember, the ones you outgrew for your stamps).

▲ There are also little round plastic containers that screw into each other. You can find these in craft stores, bead stores, fishing and hardware sections of discount stores.

Paper

Papers need to breathe, so keep your reams of paper flat. The stackable letter trays are perfect for this. Store each kind of paper in its own tray. Or put different colors together in each tray: brights, pastels, naturals, glossy, etc.

For large sheets of lighter weight paper, especially the beautiful hand-made papers and oriental papers, you can roll them and store them in individual rolls, perhaps in a tall, round wastebasket. They can also be stored flat, or hung over some type of horizontal storage poles, such as a drying rack.

Keep a plastic drawer or box to throw in all your paper scraps. Ones that have been cut and are scraps, as well as pretty pieces of small papers you may find. Look for transparent papers, floral bags, wallpaper scraps, wrapping paper, Sunday comics, etc. You never know when something in this drawer may inspire you, or when you'll need just a certain color or patterned paper to complete a project.

Keep another plastic drawer or box for your "mistakes." If you're stamping something and smudge it, or it doesn't look right, or it's not working, put it in the drawer. There are many times when something in this drawer will work great as an add-on to what you're doing. Often, you can cut a small part out of a larger "mistake" and recycle it.

For Inspiration

Besides a drawer with paper scraps, and a drawer with usuable mistakes, I also have a drawer that I throw in magazine pictures of any unusual compositions. I have greeting cards in here that have great design combinations, or unusual techniques, clever compositions, or some type of a pop-up that might work with stamping.

These are never-ending sources of inspiration. Everytime you look at an idea you saved, you will find something new in that idea to inspire you all over again. Stampers often tell me they have no "original" ideas. That they have to "copy" something someone else did, or something they saw. However, even when you think you are copying an idea, your own style will add a new twist to the original. Every artist derives inspiration from the things around, so don't think of "copying," think of "inspiration!" An inspiration drawer is a wonderful place to save things that are pleasing to you.

I also have a bookshelf filled with books. There are technique books on art, crafts, folding, calligraphy, as well as inspirational books of drawings, kids books, design books. Inspiration can hit you from everything you surround yourself with.

▲ ▲ ▲

A Rubber Room of Our Own

With the number of our stamps increasing, just think how wonderful it would be to have a room dedicated for our stamping. There have been many discussions of what we would want in our own rubber room. It is fun to fantasize, and this can give us ideas for storage, even if we don't have a complete room for ourselves.

Ideas
Here are some things that I have wanted, and others have said they want when talking about the perfect space. This may give you ideas of what you can do to make your stamping space more efficient and inspiring.

- ▲ Lots of drawers for stamps and accessories.
- ▲ Lots of shelving for:
  - stamps
  - paper
  - supplies
- ▲ Plenty of good light.
- ▲ Bookcases for books and ideas, computer software.
- ▲ A cork wall to pin up mail art, instructions, addresses, ideas.
- ▲ File drawers for catalogs and information.
- ▲ TV and video player to watch instructional tapes.
- ▲ Photocopier.
- ▲ Paper cutter...both a large one, and a personal trimmer.
- ▲ Drafting table.
- ▲ Light box.

▲ ▲ ▲

Cataloging

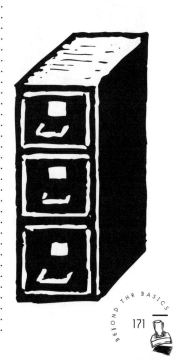

Besides storing our stamps in some type of system so we can find stamps when we need them, we can also use a catalog system to see all the images we own. This is absolutely not necessary to the art of stamping. However, if you spend much time looking for a particular stamp, or want to know if you have a certain stamp from a specific company, a catalog may be what you need.

A catalog can be used to see what we have and what we might be missing (aren't we always needing something to "fill in!"). It is also a great source of inspiration. Often, just looking through our images, we'll see one that is just "calling" to us. Or perhaps it's the juxtaposition of stamps in the book that will give us a new idea.

I often use my book before I buy new stamps to make sure I

don't already have the stamp. Once, on vacation, I bought the same stamp from the same store two days in a row!!! And I have bought many duplicates without my book at hand. At least, I'm consistent in what I like!

Use a notebook.

▲ I started with a beautiful bound ledger. Not smart! Remember, our stamps GROW!

▲ The first decision is whether you want to catalog your stamps by stamp company or by category. I, of course, like doing it by company (remember, I'm the one who can buy the same stamp over and over). I store my stamps by category, but catalog them by company. Others like to categorize them in their notebook as well. This makes it easy to find just the right stamp when working on an idea. Some people who stamp their designs out by category put the name of the stamp company below each image on the sheet.

▲ Use a 3-ring binder and plastic page protectors. Using any type of paper (typing paper will work), label the top of your page the way you want to categorize your stamps. By company, each page will have the name of an individual stamp company on top. By category, the pages will each have a different category.

• Stamp out your stamp collection. You can stamp randomly on the paper, or number the images, make columns, whatever. Slip each sheet into a plastic page protector and into the binder. You will probably want to arrange the categories alphabetically in your notebook.

• You can keep track of colors of stamp pads, markers, embossing powders as well. Use one sheet for stamp pad colors. Take one of your simpler stamps, such as a heart, star, or squiggle, and stamp it in each pad color on the paper. Especially with rainbow pads, you may want to write below it what the name of the pad is. You

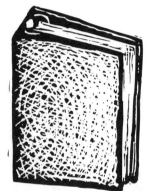

can do the same with markers and embossing powders as well.

- You might want to keep a page in the back of the book with the names and addresses of stamp companies, as well as local stamp stores, and other sources you may need.
- The Stamper's Log™, by Epilog Designs, is a 3-ring binder that has all the pages printed and ready to stamp, It also has tabs for dividing the catagories, and pre-printed category lists.

▲ Store your *masks* and your stamp positioner *positioning papers* here, as well. Behind each page in your binder, you can have something that will hold the masks and positioning papers for the images stamped on that page.

- Put them in a separate page protector.
- Use a manilla envelope, punched to fit the binder.
- Clear plastic pages with pockets, used for baseball cards, photos, negatives, etc. can be used for this purpose.
- Three-ring album pages that have plastic covers that peel back, with a sticky page inside. These will keep the masks in place, and you will be able to see what you have.

▲ Stamp your images on pieces of transparent acetate sheets. Use these as masks. You can also flip through your stamping book, holding the overlays to get ideas of how images will work together. Or, tape them to the monitor when playing with stamps and text on the computer. (See *Computers.*)

By Computer

You could also catalog your stamp collection by entering it on a database on your computer. You will not have your images on the screen unless you have a scanner and want to scan in all your stamps. But you can put the stamp name, stamp

Categories
Categories
Categories

- people ✓
- postoids
- birds B ✓ Big
- inside ✓ outside
- scenery ✓
- children
- the sea
- holidays ✓
-
- music
-
- frames, music
- mortises
- rebus
- insects Big
-
- scenery
-
- trees / fruit / water

- animals ♥
- birthday
- water
- related
- textures
-
- women
- causes
- nature
-
- special occasion
- jars & bottles ✓
- art
- famous
- people
- sea/water
-
- containers ✓
-
- architecture
- Halloween
- words Big
-
- people-single
- men
- circus
- food & drink
-
- space
-
- body parts

- cows
- cartoon
- characters
- walls,
- fences
-
- scenery
- Christmas
- inanimate objects
- people-groups
- crowds
- furniture
- abstract / graphics
- graphics
- fantasy
-
- alphabets / hearts / stars
-
- hearts
- sun/sky
-
- flowers
-
- ethnic

company, and if you wish, the date you bought the stamp. This would give you an inventory of all your stamps.

Mural

You may want a stamped mural instead of a book. This would assume you have a permanent place to hang this near your stamps, and your stamping.

▲ Stamp all your stamps on a loooong piece of newsprint, or banner paper.
▲ Stamp in categories, and pin the mural on the wall.
▲ When you buy a new stamp, just stamp it in its section, then add it to its drawer.
▲ You can see everything you have at once. When you need to look for "go together" images they'll be right in front of you.
▲ You could also find a stamp in its category if you can't remember how you categorized it when you put it away!
▲ The mural can serve as inspiration in your stamping.

This may sound like an awful lot of work for a pastime that's supposed to be enjoyable. It will take time when you begin. It depends on how far along you are in your stamp collecting when you decide to do this. You may never have a need for it, and in that case, don't even bother.

If you have been collecting stamps, and finally decide now is the time to categorize your stamps into some type of book:
▲ Take one drawer at a time, and stamp out every stamp in a single drawer.
▲ Then put that drawer, or container, etc. back, and begin a new one.
▲ You needn't do your whole collection at once; just make sure you do the entire container before putting it back.
▲ Once you have finished with your existing collection, you need to remain diligent and stamp a new design into your book before you allow yourself to put the stamp away. This

is not that hard to do. And, if you find anything wrong with the stamp—it needs to be trimmed, or even perhaps, it is not made right, and you need to return it—you will know right away.

If you use masks or use a stamp positioner often, you may want to make a mask and a positioning paper for the stamp at the same time. This is a real time-saver when you are creating. Put the mask and positioning paper in the envelope or page behind the image.

Traveling with Stamps

You may want to take some of your stamps along on vacation. It is very relaxing to have stamping you can do in your hotel room. It's also a great way to keep kids busy, especially if you have an unexpected, rainy day during your stay. On business trips, stamping can be a wonderful way to relieve stress and unwind.

Not only can you stamp in the hotel room, at the resort, at your relative's home, etc., you can also do some stamping while you're flying! A nice cross-country, or overseas flight, can be made very pleasant if you pass the time stamping. Even car travel can accomodate stamping.

Things to consider packing for travel:
▲ A flat surface to work on.
▲ Scrap paper. A small newsprint tablet works well as both scrap paper and a flat surface.
▲ Stamp cleaner in a spray or roll-on bottle, or
▲ Baby wipes to clean your stamps and your hands.
▲ A basic stamp pad. Put a rubber band around the pad while in transit.
▲ Markers.
▲ Stamps you want to play with.
▲ Cardstock.
▲ Correction fluid or sticker paper can save drastic mistakes. (Like hitting an airpocket!)
▲ Zippered baggies to store stamps that are dirty, bottles that might spill.
▲ Post-it notes.
▲ Anything else you need (such as a ruler, X-Acto knife).
▲ A good traveling container. Perhaps a fishing tackle box, or a hinged plastic box will work well.

If you are in a swap, or owe some stamped art, this is the perfect time to get some of this done. Before you leave, take the names and addresses of those you're sending to. Don't forget envelopes and stamps. If it's a swap, bring along the instructions. You might stamp out the card once the way you are going to do it for the swap before you leave home. Then you can bring the right stamps and accessories with you!

In the case of stamping, it's not true that you can't take it with you!!!

▲ ▲ ▲

Stamp Conventions

Just a few years ago, if you wanted to go to a stamp convention, you needed to travel to California. Now, conventions are popping up across the country.

A stamp convention is a fascinating and wonderful place to go. You will be surrounded by thousands of rubber lovers, just as yourself. You will be surprised at the number of people that are interested in the same things you are.

Generally, the conventions, wherever they are held, have many things in common.

▲ Usually from 30-50 or more stamp companies have their own booth at the convention.

▲ They have all their stamps and accessories displayed and on sale. Even if you have lots of good stamp stores in your areas, you will not be able to see a stamp company's entire line of stamps all spread out before you, as you will at a convention.

▲ Stamp companies generally sell their catalogs at their booths.

▲ The rubber stamp periodicals each have a booth. This allows you to see what magazines are available, and gives you a chance to subscribe, often at a discount.

- ▲ Many booths run demos, demonstrating the use of their stamps, giving you new ideas, and new techniques.
- ▲ Most conventions offer free mini-seminars or classes, teaching new techniques and ideas.
- ▲ This is where you can find unmounted rubber dies, and grab bags of unmounted rubber.
- ▲ You will find that the convention-goers are all friendly, love to talk to each other and exchange rubber ideas.

▲ ▲ ▲

- ▲ Bring along a large, sturdy canvas bag to carry your purchases. It is too hard to carry around a lot of little individual bags, and you may lose them that way. Most conventions sell bags with the convention logo on them.
- ▲ Wear comfortable clothes for digging through the rubber die piles.
- ▲ Bring plenty of cash! Companies don't always take plastic, and it's very time-consuming to write checks.
- ▲ Take along a very light-weight camera if you want to take pictures of sample cards on display in the booths. (Be sure to get permission first!)
- ▲ Carry a mirror with you if you are thinking of buying unmounted rubber dies. There will be no indexed mounts to see what the image looks like. Word stamps, especially, are hard to read backwards.
- ▲ There are often good buys on wood and mounting cushion.
- ▲ Check over the prepackaged bags of wood to be sure they are the size you'll need.
- ▲ Time goes very fast at these conventions, even if you're going to be there from open to close.
- ▲ Drinks and lunch are usually for sale. To avoid long lines and high prices:
  - • Pack your car with a cooler filled with drinks and food.
  - • Make plans with friends. Organize a pot luck lunch

Convention tips

where you can meet and share your purchases. Each of you have exciting finds to share, and you will still have time to take advantage of what you missed. ▲

Index